M000307442

AUTOBIOGRAPHY OF AN EX-WHITE MAN

AUTOBIOGRAPHY OF AN EX-WHITE MAN

LEARNING A NEW MASTER NARRATIVE FOR AMERICA

Robert Paul Wolff

 UNIVERSITY OF ROCHESTER PRESS

First published 2005
Reprinted in paperback 2009
Transferred to digital printing 2010

University of Rochester Press
668 Mt. Hope Avenue, Rochester, NY 14620, USA
www.urpress.com
and Boydell & Brewer Limited
PO Box 9, Woodbridge, Suffolk IP12 3DF, UK
www.boydellandbrewer.com

Hardcover ISBN-10: 1–58046–180–8
Paperback ISBN-10: 1–58046–313–4
Paperback ISBN-13: 978–1–58046–313–3

Library of Congress Cataloging-in-Publication Data

Wolff, Robert Paul.
   Autobiography of an ex-white man : learning a new master narrative for
America / Robert Paul Wolff.
      p. cm.
   Includes bibliographical references and index.
   ISBN 1-58046-180-8 (hardcover : alk. paper)
      1. African Americans–Study and teaching. 2. African Americans–Historiography. 3.
African American philosophy. 4. African Americans–Civil rights. 5. United States–Race
relations. 6. University of Massachusetts at Amherst. W.E.B. DuBois Dept. of Afro-
American Studies. 7. Wolff, Robert Paul. 8. Whites–Massachusetts–Amherst–Biography.
9. College teachers–Massachusetts–Amherst–Biography. 10. Philosophers–
Massachusetts–Amherst–Biography. I. Title.
E184.7.W65 2004
973'.0496073'007202–dc22
                                                        2004021545

A catalogue record for this title is available from the British Library.

This publication is printed on acid-free paper.

Jacket design: Lisa Mauro

For

Niyi, Ernie, John, Femi, Archie, Manisha, Jim, Nelson, Dorrance, Yemisi,
Bill, Esther, Mike, and Steve

and for

Brandon, Njûbi, Michael, Tanya, Hilton, Gail, and Kenny
Jennifer, Carolyn, Andrew, Rita, and Chris
Tkweme, Takao, Alesia, Dan, Dave, Lloren, and Shawn
Catherine, Zeb, Adam, Trimiko, and Stephanie
Paul, Marieta, Sandra, and Mark
Ousmane, Mirei, Christy, Angie, and Karla
Tom, Keli, Ada, Lindsey, and Anthony
Angie, Jackie, Jamal, Chris, and David
James, Allia, McKinley, Matthew, and David
And Tricia

but especially

for Esther

Yet it cannot be so embarrassing for a coloured man to be taken for white as for a white man to be taken for coloured; and I have heard of several cases of the latter kind.

—James Weldon Johnson, *The Autobiography of an Ex-Coloured Man*, Chapter 10

CONTENTS

ACKNOWLEDGMENTS

This little book bears more than the usual burden of debts. As the opening chapter makes clear, I am more deeply in debt to my colleagues in the W. E. B. Du Bois Department of Afro-American Studies at the University of Massachusetts Amherst than I can ever fully acknowledge or repay. To several of them, I owe a very special word of thanks. Mike Thelwell cast his basilisk eye on the first chapter, and suggested a large number of essential changes that, in his wise words, "saved me from grievous bodily harm." Bill Strickland and Manisha Sinha read an early draft of the entire book, and most of their suggestions have been incorporated into the text.

It is one of the empty conceits of the academic world that one learns as much from one's students as one teaches them. In my case, I think this is quite literally true for the forty-eight students who have entered our doctoral program in its first nine years. Two of those students—Shawn Alexander and Andrew Rosa—did yeoman work hunting up sources, quotes, and books for my use in the writing of the second chapter. Shawn has now returned to his important work on Black intellectual history of the turn of the twentieth century, and Andrew continues what will be a ground-breaking dissertation on St. Clair Drake. Yet another outstanding student, Jennifer Jensen-Wallach, read the manuscript and encouraged me to bring it to publication at a time when I was having doubts. I am very grateful for her faith in me.

My good friend, Professor Adrian Piper, with whom I share a dedication to the thought of Immanuel Kant, knows far more than I can ever learn about what it means to be Black in America, and she took time from the preparation of her monumental three-volume work on rationality to read my words and steer me clear of certain rocks and shoals.

My younger son, Professor Tobias Wolff, whose bailiwick is the law, solved a very difficult expositional problem for me virtually instantaneously over the phone—yet one more evidence of his wisdom and insight.

Authors frequently thank their literary agents in these prefatory acknowledgments. Never having had an agent, I had no idea what such a person might actually do for an author. This time around, I decided to sign up with a literary agency, and through the intermediation of my old friend, Jane Mansbridge, got in touch with Ike Williams. I went to him with a variety of projects, one of which included an essay on my experiences in an Afro-American Studies department, and it was he who had the idea of turning that essay into a book. It was an inspired suggestion, offered almost in passing over lunch, and I am very grateful to him for it. Ike turned the project over to his associate, Brettne Bloom, who was an inexhaustible spring of encouragement, good cheer, and detailed editorial emendations. It comes as something of a surprise to find myself saying this, but I honestly think that without Ike and Brettne, this book would not exist.

I don't usually thank copyeditors, since in the forty years that I have been writing books, my experiences with them have been more unhappy than not, but this time around, I was blessed with a dream editor. Louise Goldberg handled my manuscript with intelligence and taste, and gave me help with permissions and such that can only be called supererogatory. What is more, she turns out to share with me a love for the viola. We have become friends, through our many email communications. Meeting her has been one of the unexpected pleasures of publishing with the University of Rochester Press.

And a special thanks to my fellow anarchist, Tim Madigan. Tim has left the Press to resume teaching philosophy. It is a loss for the press, but a gain for his students.

As the first endnote to Chapter Two indicates, I am indebted to Ms. Padge Jordan of Houghton Mifflin for graciously making available to me a number of editions of Thomas Bailey's American History textbook.

I am grateful to the following publishers for permission to quote from their books: Houghton Mifflin: Bailey's *The American Pageant*; Oxford University Press: Morrison and Commager's *The Growth of the American Republic* and Nevin and Commager's *America: The Story of a Free People*. The passages from W. E. B. Du Bois's *Black Reconstruction in America, 1860–1880* are reprinted with the permission of Scribner, an imprint of Simon & Schuster Adult Publishing Group (Copyright © 1935, 1962 by W. E. Burghardt Du Bois).

I am also indebted to the anonymous reader for the University of Rochester Press, who read the manuscript with intelligence and sympathy and made several valuable suggestions, which I have incorporated into the text.

Finally, a personal word of affection for my wife, Susan, who accepted with characteristic good cheer my incomprehensible decision to leave philosophy and transfer to an Afro-American Studies department, and who has joined with me in the great adventure narrated in these pages.

PREFACE

This is the story of a journey—not in space or in time, but in understanding. It has been for me a journey both exhilarating and humbling: exhilarating because on this journey I have learned much that before was closed to me; humbling, because on this journey I discovered how blind I had been to a world that I thought I understood.

Kierkegaard observes somewhere—I think it is in the *Concluding Unscientific Postscript*—that just as it is harder to jump into the air and land exactly on the spot from which you took off, so it is more difficult to become a Christian when you have the misfortune to have been born a Christian. I faced just such a problem with regard to the subject of race in America. Before I began my journey, I thought of myself as a sensitive, knowledgeable, politically committed advocate of racial justice. But as I took the first steps along the way, I began to realize that I understood little or nothing at all about that color line called by W. E. B. Du Bois the problem of the twentieth century. So, rather like the conventional Christian who seeks to become truly a Christian, my task was to undergo a difficult process of reeducation and self-examination, in order to end up where I thought I had begun—as a committed advocate of racial justice. Perhaps I can take comfort from Socrates' teaching that the first step of the journey toward wisdom is the acknowledgment that one is ignorant.

I did not set out on my journey deliberately, with forethought and planning. It began as a lark, a *jeu d'esprit*. Only after I was well begun did I even realize what I was doing, and what was happening to me. Twelve years ago, after a long career as a Professor of Philosophy, I was unexpectedly invited to join an Afro-American Studies Department in order to participate in the effort to create a ground-breaking doctoral program. I was bored with Philosophy and very unhappy in my home department, which was a narrow, unfriendly, unenlightened place, so I jumped at the chance for what sounded like an interesting change of pace. I had no inkling that before too many years had gone by, my whole way of seeing the world would change.

This short book tells the story of how I was helped by my new colleagues and by my students to see America through their eyes. I have tried not only to describe the process of enlightenment, but also to put into words, as well as I can, the new vision of America that I finally achieved. To some readers—certainly to those who are Black—this will be old news. But I think there are many thoughtful, progressive, well-meaning Americans whose eyes are as closed as mine were to the real story of America. This book is meant especially for them.

Even now, after twelve years spent officially as a Professor of Afro-American Studies, I am no sort of scholar at all of the subject. I have made no new archival discoveries, crafted no new readings of literary texts, arrived at no understandings of race in America that were not already voiced by scholars, activists, and other observers. But I have come to believe that my own personal journey may provide some signposts for others who are willing to set out on a similar journey.

I will tell a story I have learned—a new Master Narrative for all of America. It is very different from the story we have all learned in school, at Fourth of July celebrations, and in countless political speeches. It lacks the comfortable self-congratulation of which we are all so fond. But it is a true story, and I believe only the truth can set us free.

I will also explain why I have come to believe that among the many bearers and tellers of this story, a special place should be reserved for those scholars and teachers who work and write in Black Studies Departments at America's colleges and universities.

North America is now in its fifth century of racial oppression and injustice. Even the most undaunted optimists, among whom I count myself, must surely grant that things are not going to be all right if we are just patient. Only concerted, unrelenting action for racial justice will change half a millennium of injustice. I am mindful of the young Karl Marx's call to arms in his famous Eleventh Thesis on Feuerbach: "The philosophers have *only* interpreted the world, in various ways; the point, however, is to *change* it." I think Marx would agree that we can succeed in changing the world only if we understand it. It is my hope that this slender volume will make a contribution to that understanding.

1

AUTOBIOGRAPHY OF AN EX-WHITE MAN

The books piled up on the coffee table until they threatened to block the view of my living room. Fifty-three books, twenty thousand pages of African-American history, politics, fiction, essays, and poetry. It was the first day of June 1996, and I had to read them all by September 3rd. On that day, seven eager young Black men and women would show up at New Africa House on the University of Massachusetts campus, ready to start a demanding new doctoral program in Afro-American Studies. We would require them in the first year to read all fifty-three books and write a paper on each one. They would look to me as Graduate Program Director for guidance, encouragement, and wisdom, and there I sat, knowing next to nothing about the history, the trials, the triumphs, the artistic creations, the experiences of Black folk in America.

My field was Philosophy, not Afro-Am, and at that moment, I probably knew less about the discipline of Afro-American Studies than one of our undergraduate majors. I thought that my politics were impeccable, my commitments clear. I had managed an anti-apartheid organization of Harvard graduates for two years, and for the past six years, I had run a little one-man scholarship organization raising money for poor Black university students in South Africa. I had picketed Woolworth's in the sixties, supporting the young Black students who started the modern Civil Rights Movement with their sit-in in Greensboro. But I knew virtually nothing about slavery, Reconstruction, share-cropping, Black Codes, Jim Crow, the Harlem Renaissance, the World War I riots, or the Black Arts Movement.

I am a slow, methodical reader, incapable of skimming lightly through a book. This is fine if you are going to be a philosopher. Close

1

reading of a small number of famous texts is what philosophers do. I often pointed out to my students during my days as a Professor of Philosophy that you could get a pretty fair education as a student of philosophy by mastering perhaps twenty-five or thirty texts from the Western tradition. Indeed, if you were willing to treat all of Plato's Dialogues as one enormous book, you could probably bring the list down to twenty titles. So the mountain of volumes awaiting me was daunting indeed. It was going to be a long summer.

I sighed, and reached for the first book on the pile. It was the seventh edition of John Hope Franklin's classic work, *From Slavery to Freedom*. I didn't take notes. I just read carefully one book after another, in the order prescribed by our syllabus, making marginal comments, as I have always done. My goal was to immerse myself in them, so that I would have a grasp of the overarching shape of the story of Black Americans.

As the title suggests, Franklin's work is an upbeat history of African Americans, beginning with the torment of the Middle Passage and slavery, and taking the reader out of that darkness and into the sunlight of freedom. First published in 1947, the text has been revised again and again to incorporate the tribulations of postwar Jim Crow, the triumph of *Brown v. Board of Education*, the drama of the Civil Rights Movement, and the struggles over affirmative action. Every page is filled with names, dates, and events about which I knew next to nothing.

John Hope Franklin is the Dean of African-American historians, held in the highest esteem by younger Black historians, many of whom he trained at Chicago and Duke. In a profession that for generations did not even acknowledge the Black presence in America, save in the most dismissive and abusive of terms, John Hope had to struggle to gain any sort of professional recognition. Eventually, his White colleagues were forced to admit the weight of his scholarly contributions, and elected him the first Black President of the Southern Historical Association, the Organization of American Historians, and the American Historical Association. I knew none of this on that day in June. To me, the book was just the first in a large pile waiting to be read.

After plowing through Franklin, I read a collection of four famous slave narratives, edited by Henry Louis Gates, Jr., and followed that with *Black History and the Historical Profession, 1915–1980*, by August Meier and Elliott Rudwick. This last work struck me as an odd pairing with the Franklin and Gates, but my colleague John Henry Bracey, Jr. was the protegé of Augie Meier, and later his collaborator on a number of scholarly essays and editorial collections, so it seemed that we were engaging in the time-honored academic practice of introducing our students to those who had been our own mentors.

I read on. Eric Williams' *Capitalism and Slavery* is a classic thesis book about the role of Caribbean slavery in the growth of British capitalism. Originally his doctoral dissertation, it argues the striking and controversial thesis that the growth of British industry was funded by the profits from the slave trade and the sale of slave-produced Caribbean sugar. *Black Majority* by Peter Wood, another classic work, focuses on the early period of slavery in South Carolina. This is a natural successor to the Williams, because of the important link between Barbados and South Carolina during the eighteenth century. Reading the book, I learned for the first time of the hideous practice of "seasoning" newly captured Africans in Barbados—which is to say beating them into submission—before selling them to South Carolinian plantation owners. Peter is an old friend of mine from my struggles against apartheid at Harvard, and I was delighted to encounter him in the pile.

Early in the summer, I read Herbert Gutman's *The Black Family in Slavery and Freedom*, written by Gutman as a response to Patrick Moynihan's notorious "benign neglect" memorandum on the African-American family. Through the sort of painstaking archival scholarship that Moynihan did not trouble himself with, Gutman demonstrated that against all the odds, in the face of the brutality and disruptions of slavery, Africans and their descendants had created and maintained strong family units. Often, they were forced to counter the destructive effects of slave sales by substituting extended kin relations for those of the nuclear family. If a father or mother was sold down the river, an "aunt" or "uncle" would step in to take over the burdens of child-rearing. This practice of kin caring for children continues down to the present day, putting the lie to Moynihan's claim that the economic troubles of Negroes are due to an absence of what are today called "family values."

As the weeks passed, I became more and more absorbed by my reading. Some of the historical works were fascinating and beautifully written. Judge A. Leon Higgenbotham's *In the Matter of Color* deals with the law of slavery in six of the American colonies prior to the Revolutionary war. For the first time, I learned something of the extraordinary complexity of the early attempts by judges and lawyers to find in the English Common Law some justification for the racial oppression of chattel slavery.

I was ravished by the outpouring of vivid contemporary detail in Leon Litwack's *Been in the Storm So Long*, an astonishing book about the ways in which the slaves experienced and reacted to liberation at the end of the Civil War. In Litwack's pages, the slaves and freed people began to come alive to me as individuals, with passions, skills, and a fully developed ironic understanding of their own situation. More perhaps than any other single work in the pile, this book weaned me away from my tendency to look *at* Black men and women rather than to look at the world *through* their eyes.

Some of the books were solid, workmanlike monographs, useful for fleshing out the story of the African-American experience: Gary Nash's *Forging Freedom*, a portrait of free Blacks in Philadelphia; *They Who Would Be Free*, by Jane and William Pease, telling the story of Black abolitionists. Another old friend from anti-apartheid days, Nell Painter, turned up with *Exodusters*, her account of the migration of freedmen and women from the South to Kansas in the years just after the Civil War.

Later in the summer, I worked my way into the twentieth century, reading *Black Metropolis* by St. Clair Drake and Horace Cayton, a massive work, more than eight hundred pages long. This is a classic sociological study of the Black community in Chicago, one of the first major works of urban sociology. Only years later would I learn that Drake had been one of John Bracey's teachers, and a major figure in Pan-African and American Negro political movements. For the moment, I was content to learn something about the Black community in the South Side of Chicago, which I had lived next to but had never explored during my two years at the University of Chicago.

The literary half of the list started slowly, with *Clotel, Iola Leroy, The Conjure Woman*, and *Uncle Tom's Cabin* representing pre–Civil War fictions. *Clotel*, a novel by an escaped slave, William Wells Brown, is based on the belief widely held in the Black community that Thomas Jefferson had fathered mulatto children by one of his slaves. It took the miracles of modern science to demonstrate to the White community that the oral traditions of Blacks are frequently more reliable than the written assurances of established scholars.

Near the end of the summer, I read *Their Eyes Were Watching God* and *Jonah's Gourd Vine* by Zora Neale Hurston, *Native Son* and *Uncle Tom's Children* by Richard Wright, *Invisible Man* by Ralph Ellison, *If He Hollers Let Him Go* by Chester Himes, and *Go Tell It on The Mountain* by James Baldwin. Our students were in for a treat!

I was so absorbed in the enterprise of reading this huge stack of books—checking off titles, shifting volumes one by one from the to-read to the already-read pile—that for much of the summer, I did not take the time to reflect on the experience I was undergoing, but slowly, little by little, as I drew closer to the end of the list, I began to realize that something quite remarkable was happening to me, something I had not anticipated when I began my labors.

This was actually the third time in my life that I had attempted a concentrated bout of reading of this magnitude. The first time had been in the spring of 1958, when I read the major works of Western political theory, and then went on to read twenty thousand pages of European history in preparation for teaching Freshman history at Harvard. The second time had been just twenty years later, when I immersed myself for a sabbatical semester in theoretical economics so that I could master the modern mathematical reinterpretation of the economic theories of Karl Marx. Each of these efforts had greatly broadened the scope of my knowledge and insight, but neither had in any fundamental way changed me. I was the same radical philosopher after the political theory, history, and economics that I had been before.

But as the story of the African-American experience washed over me in all its horrible and glorious detail, the very structure of my perception and conception of America underwent an irreversible alteration. I saw everything differently—I saw the Puritans differently, and I saw Rodney King differently; I saw the Civil War differently, and I saw O. J. Simpson differently. I saw my colleagues differently; I even saw myself differently. By the time the summer was over and nothing remained in the pile of books to be read save *The Negro Caravan* [which I never did manage to plow through], I found myself living in a world I had never before inhabited, seeing the world through entirely new eyes.

How exactly had my perceptions, my conceptions, and I myself changed? It is not so easy to put the changes into words. In a way, this entire book is my attempt to say, clearly and explicitly, what I felt rather inchoately at the end of that summer of intensive reading.

The change was not merely a matter of accumulated information. I now knew about the Stono Rebellion, and I understood the structure of the triangular trade that circulated slaves, raw materials, and finished goods among Europe, West Africa, and North America. I had for the first time some feel for the complex detail of the laws governing slavery in the Colonies and then in the United States prior to the Civil War. Perhaps most important of all, I understood that the long, painful saga of Black men and women in America was not a story of slow, steady improvement, but rather an endless repetition of hopes raised and then dashed, of advances followed by brutal reversals. But facts were not the substance of what had happened to me, though they played a role, to be sure. Rather,

I was for the first time beginning to see America from the standpoint of African Americans. Let us be clear. I was still, as I had been and am now, a New York Jewish professor from a non-religious middle-class family. I was under no illusions about being Black or thinking Black. But because I had made the life choice to change my departmental affiliation, with everything that meant, I found myself beginning to be able to see how the world might look to my colleagues. And it was starting to look the same way to me.

I think more than anything else my perceptions were altered by the sheer repetition of detail in the books I had read—the fictions as well as the historical accounts. Reading about one whipping or one lynching is upsetting. Reading statistics of the numbers of whippings or lynchings is an education. But reading description after description, in book after book, of maimings, killings, whippings, and lynchings in the seventeenth century, the eighteenth century, the nineteenth century, and the twentieth century made me finally understand why so many of my colleagues seemed deeply, irreversibly pessimistic about the prospects for anything resembling racial justice. To them—and, by the end of the summer, to me as well—the beating of Rodney King was neither remarkable nor unexpected. It was an episode that was continuous with almost four centuries of oppression.

The images of the fictions blended in my imagination with the factual accounts dredged from archives by historians. The Battle Royal in *Invisible Man*, the lynching in *Uncle Tom's Children*, the bitter unfairness of the ending of *If He Hollers Let Him Go* were no more terrible, no more implausible, indeed no more powerfully realized in their literary settings, than the purely factual accounts of the Negro who was lynched on the stage of a theater before Whites who had paid to see the show.

Stories have a power to shape our experience, to impose interpretations on what we think we know—both true stories and fictional ones. The story of America organizes our collective social memory, highlighting turning points, bringing some facts into sharp focus, concealing others. If our national story is told wrongly, we shall forget our real past, and then—because stories have this power—we shall misunderstand our present and lose the ability to shape our future. Freud says somewhere that if there is any one subject that it is not permitted to discuss in an analysis, sooner or later the entire analysis comes to be about that one subject. Race is the dirty little secret of the American story—not greed, not sex, not power. Until the American story is rewritten with the fact of slavery and its aftermath given its true place, none of us in the White community will be able to understand the story of America aright.

I am a White seventy-year-old New York Jewish intellectual. What on earth am I doing in a Black Studies department?

I was educated in philosophy at Harvard in the early fifties, where I studied with the logician Willard van Orman Quine, the epistemologist Clarence Irving Lewis, and the great medievalist scholar Harry Austryn Wolfson. I started out to be a logician, moved on to the study of the philosophy of Immanuel Kant [to this day, the license plate on my car is "I KANT"], went from there to political philosophy, and then to Karl Marx's economic theories—pretty much the road to Hell as things were viewed back in those days.

I grew up in Queens in a non-religious home. When I was twelve, my mother told me that I was the product of a mixed marriage. "Your father is an agnostic and I am an atheist," she said. "All the other boys are going to go to Hebrew school, get bar mitzvah'd, have a big party and get lots of presents. You can do that, or your father and I will give you a hundred dollars and you can get yourself something." I took the hundred and bought Natie Gold's set of model trains, which I coveted. That was my last encounter with organized religion.

The politics in my home were a curious mixture of hatred and piety. My father hated Communists, he hated Zionists, and—though the connection is somewhat tenuous—he hated the Board of Education, for whom he worked as a science teacher and then High School principal. The piety was simple enough—my mother and father voted the straight Democratic ticket, and it never crossed their minds, or the minds of any of their friends, to consider voting for a Republican. My aunt and uncle were friendly with one light-skinned upper middle class Black couple, but I think my parents figured that was quite enough broad-minded outreach by the extended family.

I began my political life as a Truman supporter in 1948, and have drifted steadily to the left as I have grown older. Marx and Engels had a little private joke they liked to repeat in their correspondence. They would say that they got their philosophy [or religion] from the Germans, their politics from the French, and their economics from the English. I have always thought that if you knew someone's stand on religion, politics, and economics, you could pretty well tell where he or she would be on any important issue, so when people ask me what I believe, I say I am an atheist in religion, an anarchist in politics, and a Marxist in economics.

During most of my life, I have had progressive opinions on matters of race, but little or no personal experience or understanding of the real dynamics of race in America. To be sure, I picketed Woolworth after the

Greensboro sit-ins. But my closest connection with the Black community in America came in the early sixties, when I served for a time in an all-Black Army National Guard regiment in Chicago. This requires a little explanation, for those of you too young to remember the draft.

Back when I was a teenager, in the aftermath of World War II, all men were required to register for the draft when they reached eighteen. The Army actually got around to calling you when you were twenty-one or twenty-two, but if you were in college, you could get a deferment until you graduated. If you went on to graduate school, you could keep getting deferments until you reached the magic age of twenty-six, at which point, even though you continued legally to be eligible up to thirty-five, the Army wouldn't call you. For this reason, almost no one with a graduate degree from my generation served in the Army.

But I was precocious, alas. By the time I received a draft notice, just before my twenty-second birthday in December 1956, I was six months away from finishing my doctorate. I got my draft board to postpone my order of induction so that I could get my degree that next spring, and before they could draft me again, I joined the Massachusetts National Guard. In June, I walked with my bright crimson robe in the commencement ceremonies, and then went off to Fort Dix to do basic training.

I owed the government five and a half years of Guard meetings after my six months on active duty. I did the first three and a half years at Harvard, where I was an Instructor in Philosophy and General Education. Then, in 1961, I got an Assistant Professorship at the University of Chicago, and transferred to the nearest Guard unit, which was an all-Black regiment in the heart of the Black community of South Chicago. By this time I had risen all the way to the rank of Private First Class [or Specialist 3rd Class, as they called it in the "New Army"]. At my first Guard meeting, I was assigned to Headquarters Company, where my job was to carry the equipment of the Regimental photographer, a Master Sergeant by the name of Jewell Starks.

Starks had been raised a Catholic, but was now a member of the Nation of Islam. He told me he had been one of the Black Eagles at Tuskegee during World War II—the group of Black men who were trained as fliers by the Army Air Corps. At the time, this bit of information meant very little to me, but thirty-five years later, I would gain some sense of its significance.

From the time of the Revolutionary War on, Black Americans have demanded the right to serve as soldiers, in the face of the persistent contempt heaped on them by Whites. Despite having served bravely in the

American Revolution, and having made a critically important contribution to the victory of the Northern armies during the Civil War, they have been summarily brushed aside each time the country no longer needs their blood and courage. As America's entry into the Second World War drew closer, once again Black men asked to be permitted to serve. In 1941, Franklin Delano Roosevelt gave orders that led to establishment of a program at Tuskegee University to train Black fliers—the Black Eagles. Eventually, the 99th Fighter Group and the 332nd Fighter Group, both composed of Black aviators, united to form one of the most successful and highly decorated units in the Army Air Corps. Leading bombers on air strikes over Europe, Black fliers were so effective that even racist White pilots asked that their units be protected by the 99th and 332nd.

Starks was a Master Sergeant when I knew him, so I infer that he served with the ground crews, since the fliers all held officer rank. Though I did not realize it at the time, his casual remark to me testified to his connection with a proud and ground-breaking unit. By the time I came along, of course, the integration of the Armed Forces was well under way, and all of the non-coms in my basic training camp had been either Black or Latino.

The Regiment into which I transferred had a long and proud military record, of which I was completely unaware back in 1961. The other men in the unit were Black residents of South Side Chicago. They knew all too well about the racially exclusionary policies of the University of Chicago, about its practice of buying up Hyde Park real estate so that it could turn away Black renters, *including even its own Black students.* So when a White Professor showed up from the University and was handed the job of fetching and toting for Master Sergeant Starks, it must have been a source of some ironic amusement to them.

But I was completely blind to these nuances of race and authority on the South Side of Chicago. All I knew was that I had a little patch on my arm that showed I was a Spec 3, and Starks was a Master Sergeant with almost twenty years of service. He had stripes and hash marks all the way up his arm, and to my naive anarchist mind, it seemed natural that I should take orders from him and carry his gear.

My next encounter with the matter of race occurred fifteen years later, and once again the story betrays my insensitivity at that time to the realities of race in America. The events were to bear a strange relationship to my membership in a Black Studies department.

In the intervening years, I had gone on to teach at Columbia, where I was fortunate enough to be deeply involved in the 1968 building seizures and student uprisings. Eventually, I became disenchanted with the elite Ivy League segment of the Academy, and accepted a position in the philosophy department at the University of Massachusetts, a big, rural second-tier state university. In the middle seventies, UMass was in the remarkable position of having both a Black Chancellor and a Black Provost.

The Chancellor was a widely respected geologist who had been a member of the UMass faculty for some time. The Provost was a political scientist who had been recruited in a national search from his position at Florida State University. UMass had just come to the end of a rapid and somewhat chaotic period of growth, transforming itself from a small agricultural school into a 23,000 student university. The top administrative positions had for many years been controlled by a small group of senior science professors, who more or less rotated Deanships, Provostships, and Chancellorships among themselves. Although the Chancellor was a scientist, he was not a part of that circle, and they actually formed an ad hoc "advisory"group to keep an eye on him [a group into which I was invited, I am now embarrassed to admit].

Shortly after arriving, the Provost launched an attempt to shift resources and faculty lines away from Arts and Sciences and toward the professional schools. This was hardly unusual; indeed, it was merely part of a national trend that had been going on for some years, and continues to the present day. But he moved quickly, and without elaborate consultations of the sort preferred by faculty, and very soon, massive opposition to him grew in some sectors of the campus.

Almost immediately, he alienated large segments of the campus by trying peremptorily to carry out a rather far-reaching restructuring. In the late spring of 1977 things came to a head, with a call for an extraordinary meeting of all of the faculties of the University, for the purpose of issuing a vote of no confidence in the Provost. I was asked by a group of professors opposed to the Provost to give a public speech to the hundreds of professors gathered in the campus's largest lecture hall.

This effort was unprecedented at UMass, and was fueled by a variety of motivations, some of which were racial. I registered none of this at the time. To me, this was just one more opportunity to attack authority, something I had done at Harvard as an undergraduate, at Chicago as an Assistant Professor, and at Columbia as a senior professor. I loved nothing better than to stand before a crowd and call for the resignation of a Dean, a Provost, a Chancellor, or a President. Indeed, my very first publication had been a letter to the Harvard Crimson written when I was barely seventeen, calling on President James Bryant Conant to resign.

The members of the Afro-American Studies Department knew better. Regardless of the Provost's administrative style, which some of them had serious doubts about, they saw a concerted attack to get rid of a Black Provost, in the name of academic collegiality and due process—shibboleths that had for generations been invoked to keep Black men out of positions of authority.

I was in hog heaven. I like nothing better than joining with my colleagues to rail at the powers that be. At Columbia in the midst of the uprising, I had defended the building seizures in a debate against the great historian Peter Gay during a mass meeting, and—not surprisingly—was cheered to the echo by enthusiastic students. Here was another chance to make a big public splash by denouncing someone in authority.

My opponent in the public debate on this occasion was Michael Thelwell, a tall, elegant, well-spoken, witty Jamaican who was a senior professor in the Afro-American Studies department, and had been its first Head. Thelwell is a graduate of Howard, a comrade of the late Stokely Carmichael [whose authorized biography he has just written], and during the Sixties ran the SNCC office in Washington. He is a genuine hero of the Movement, and one of the most brilliant orators I have ever heard.

Well, it was a warm spring day, and I chose to wear a white suit, one of my few bits of reasonably nice clothing. I looked like one of the plantation owners in the ball scene in *Gone with the Wind.* The larger meaning of the event was not lost on Thelwell. In a long piece published in the Black Students' newspaper under the heading, "The Savaging of the Provost: Ritual Murder Among the Humanists," he used his quite considerable rhetorical powers to excoriate those who were calling for the head of the Provost. After ridiculing the pretensions of the attackers who had invoked the sanctity of the cultural, intellectual, and aesthetic traditions of Western Civilization in their assault on the Provost, he took dead aim at me. "It would all have been infinitely more moving had there really been barbarian hordes at the doors threatening to rape 'the life of the mind,' pillage 'the spirit of a great university' and worse burn the articles of governance. Or if one did not know that the most self-righteous, smug and unctuous of the lot was himself a failed candidate for the position of provost. I am talking about Robert Paul Wolff of the philosophy department, lest there be any doubt."

It is nothing short of miraculous that, fifteen years later, I was invited to join the W. E. B. Du Bois Department of Afro-American Studies at the University of Massachusetts.

Which brings me to April 22, 1992. Esther Terry and I were having lunch at the Lord Jeffrey Amherst Inn in the middle of Amherst,

Massachusetts. Esther and I sat next to a big window, looking out on the picture postcard New England Common, drinking wine and talking. The occasion for the lunch was my appointment as Esther's Co-Director of a tiny operation at the University of Massachusetts rather grandiosely called the Institute for Advanced Study in the Humanities. This was a consolation prize awarded to me behind the scenes after I ran for the Deanship of Humanities and lost.

Esther Terry is a tiny Black woman with a radiant personality that fills any room she is in and makes everyone she meets believe that she is their best friend. When she walks through the halls of the Administration Building, Vice-Chancellors and secretaries come out of their offices to throw their arms around her and greet her. Being with her makes me feel as though I were in the train of the Queen of Sheba as she entered King Solomon's court. She is the daughter of North Carolina sharecroppers, the descendant of slaves, and has, I think, the shrewdest political mind I have ever encountered.

As a young woman at Bennett College in the fifties, Esther was one of those brave students who launched the modern Civil Rights movement with their sit-in at the Greensboro Woolworth lunch counter. Esther was there at the counter from the very first day, and she has earned the right to show her scars when veterans of the Movement gather to tell war stories.

Esther came to UMass from North Carolina to do a doctorate in Literature and Drama, and stayed to become a founding member thirty-five years ago of the W. E. B. Du Bois Department of Afro-American Studies, which she now heads. Her life has been devoted to educating, caring for, and fighting for the rights of Black students both on the UMass campus and elsewhere. Esther has spent time doing theater, and when she is in the mood, she will do wicked parodies of academics who have ticked her off.

We were supposed to be discussing Institute business, but truth to tell, there wasn't much to talk about. UMass was going through one of its periodic budget crises, and the Provost had actually wanted to close the Institute down rather than continue to come up with its twenty-thousand dollar a year budget.

As we ate, Esther talked more and more animatedly about her dream of establishing a full-scale departmentally based doctoral program in Afro-American Studies. At that point, there wasn't but one such program in the country—the Afro-Centric program created at Temple University by Molefi Asante. Esther and her colleagues were not at all sympathetic to Asante's approach, so the program of which she dreamed would be the first of its kind in the world. She talked about how difficult it had been simply to keep Afro-American Studies alive in the quarter century that had passed since the uprisings of the late sixties brought the Civil Rights Movement to northern campuses. After the initial enthusiasm of the early seventies, Black Studies had been sharply cut back across the country, with five hundred programs or more dwindling to two hundred. The UMass administration had been supportive—much more so than at most other schools—but repeated budget crises had taken their toll, and the Department was now only half as large as at its height.

Finally, after the second glass of wine, Esther looked up at me and said, "How would you like to come over and teach philosophy in Afro-American Studies?"

What could possibly have prompted so unexpected a question? Somehow, I had managed in the intervening years to redeem myself in the eyes of the members of the department. They saw something in me that perhaps I did not even see in myself—something that persuaded this proud and accomplished group of scholar-activists that I deserved to be a member of the oldest free-standing Black Studies Department in America, and that I might be able to contribute something to their plans for a ground-breaking doctoral program. I have turned this puzzle over in my mind for twelve years now, and I may never fully solve it. Perhaps it was the fact that I had been active in the anti-apartheid movement, heading up a group of Harvard graduates who were pressuring their alma mater to divest. Though I did not know it at the time, the Afro-American Studies Department and the Black Chancellor had spearheaded a successful effort to make UMass the second university in the country to divest. Almost certainly, the department decided that my enthusiasm for creating new academic programs could be put to good use in their own efforts. During my years at UMass, I had started an inter-disciplinary undergraduate social theory major and a doctoral track in social and political philosophy. Esther had served on the search committee during my unsuccessful run for the Deanship, and she had heard me speak about the great pleasure I took in working to establish new educational programs. Having roots in the traditions of the Black church, although none of them now is a believing Christian, perhaps they were simply moved by the parable of the prodigal son. But I may never know the answer, for the subject is never mentioned.

At any rate, when Esther asked her question, without missing a beat, I said, "Sure." Needless to say, not by the most generous stretch of the imagination could I claim the slightest scholarly competence in Afro-American Studies. But Esther's enthusiasm was infectious, and I immediately began spinning plans in my head of ways that I might be part of the effort to create a new doctoral program. That night I wrote a three-page single-spaced memorandum suggesting steps we could take to win approval for a doctoral program. My memorandum was appropriately tentative, because I was not sure I had really heard Esther invite me to join the department, but my excitement was obvious, and within days she called me with the news that she had won a unanimous vote of approval from her department for the invitation. It was only years later that I realized how delicately and carefully she had dropped that suggestion into the conversation, very much like an expert fly fisherman casting a Royal Nymph over a pool harboring a deep-lying trout.

Ordinarily, moving a senior professor from one department to another is a bureaucratic nightmare, requiring months or years to bring off. In this case, however, my colleagues in Philosophy were happy to see me go. Scarcely two months later the transfer was completed, and I became a Professor of Afro-American Studies. It seemed like a lark—one more change of field in a career in which I had taught classes in Philosophy, Political Science, History, and Economics Departments.

As I walked across the campus on a warm June day, I scarcely realized how completely that simple move was to transform my perception of American society, and the world's perception of me.

The office buildings at the University of Massachusetts are for the most part ugly functional structures, with neither charm nor history. Bartlett Hall, where Philosophy is housed, could pass for the regional offices of the Veterans' Administration. My new department was located on the East side of the campus in a four story brick building that was indistinguishable, architecturally, from the dormitory across the street.

As I walked up to the front steps, I saw a striking black and red wooden plaque over the door proclaiming that this was "The New Africa House." As I stepped inside, I found the walls covered with brilliant murals, painted, I later learned, by the students of my new colleague, Nelson Stevens. It was years before I was told something of the history of the building and the role it had played in the struggles of Black students and faculty on the campus.

The building had indeed originally been a dormitory, as the layout of rooms and large communal bathrooms on each floor testify. But in 1969, during a protest against the racial policies [or lack of policies] of the university, a group of Black students were chased by threatening White students back to their dormitory. The Black students barricaded themselves in the dorm, told the White students there either to join forces with them or get out, and liberated the building, declaring it to be their space. The newly formed Afro-American Studies Department responded by moving itself collectively into the now-emptied dorm, and the building became The New Africa House.

This seizure of space was symbolic of the ambitious dreams of the department, for the founding faculty were not simply seeking to establish yet another academic department. Instead, they sought to create what can only be described as an entire counter-university in which the experiences, struggles, triumphs, and wisdom of Black Americans, and more broadly of all the peoples of the African Diaspora, would take their rightful place in the Academy.

The first and most pressing need was to give the small but growing number of Black students on the campus a structure of support, counseling, and legitimation. To that end, members of the department, who had been providing these services on an ad hoc basis in addition to their normal teaching duties, created the Committee for the Collegiate Education of Black and Other Minority Students. CCEBMS [or "Sebs"], as it came to be called, began the work of overcoming the hostile and unwelcoming environment that routinely confronted Black students [and students of other minorities] when they came to UMass.

In pursuit of its dream, the department began to recruit a broad spectrum of scholars and artists. Over the next few years, historians, political scientists, anthropologists, sociologists, writers, literary critics, painters, sculptors, dancers, and musicians came on board. Simply calling the roll of the faculty in those early days gives some sense of how grand the vision was. Among those who taught in the department in the early days were jazz immortal Max Roach, Johnetta Cole, later to become President of Spelman College, sociologist William Julius Wilson, Shirley Graham Du Bois [the second wife of W. E. B.], the great James Baldwin, and Africa's most distinguished writer, Chinua Achebe. Still in the department are Jazz saxophonist Archie Shepp and Stevens, one of the founding members of the Black Arts movement.

New Africa House quickly became not a classroom building or an office building but a world. In addition to the department and CCEBMS, it soon housed a restaurant, a barbershop catering to Black customers, a radio station, and even a day care center. Old-timers tell stories of groups of six-year-olds marching up and down the steps chanting revolutionary slogans.

The memories of these struggles, of three decades of triumphs and defeats, were gathered in New Africa House as I approached it that day, though at the time I was oblivious to them.

My very first day in New Africa House was something of a revelation. I walked up to the third floor, and wandered down the hall looking for the department office. As I drew near, I heard a sound that was entirely new to me in academic surroundings: loud, unforced, hearty laughter. Not snickers, or smirks, or hedged giggles, with which I had become all too familiar during my many years in Philosophy departments, but big, healthy belly laughs. My new colleagues were clearly people confident of their accomplishments and commitments, comfortable with themselves and the world around them, free of the convolutions and status anxieties that make most university departments so ready a target for satire.

Esther wasted no time. In July, shortly after my transfer, we began work in earnest on the proposal to create a doctoral program in Afro-American Studies. Almost immediately, someone—I think it was John Bracey, Jr.—had the idea of building the program on the foundation of a required first-year seminar in which our students would read masses of classic works in Afro-American Studies and write scores of papers. In this way, we would define a core of intellectual material that would be shared by every student in the program, no matter what he or she went on to specialize in. At that first meeting, we began the exciting and exhausting task of choosing the books.

The first dispute was over how many books to require. John argued hard for one hundred, but the rest of us didn't think we could get even the best of students to read carefully one hundred scholarly works in two semesters. In the end, we agreed on fifty as a reasonable number. If the seminar met two afternoons each week during the Fall and Spring semesters, that would work out to just about one book for each meeting. A paper on each book—fifty books, fifty papers. Now began the debates over which fifty books to include.

Internal politics as well as intellectual demands dictated that we devote half the list to history and politics and the other half to literature and culture. John is an historian, and faced with the prospect of being forced to limit himself not to fifty works of history, but to a mere twenty-five, he made one last effort to expand the list to one hundred. We beat him down, and went to work.

This is perhaps as good a time as any to say a few words about the people engaged in this collective creation of a canon. My new colleagues, I learned very quickly, are an extraordinary group of people, quite unlike the members of any Philosophy department I have ever been a member of. Virtually all of them came to the University of Massachusetts from some form of radical Black activism, and a quarter of a century later, their world view, intellectual style, and personal commitments have been shaped by that origin.

Esther, as I have said, came from the sit-ins in Greensboro. John Bracey, although an academic brat [his mother taught at Howard University] with an archivist's encyclopedic knowledge of documents, texts, and sources in Black history, came out of a Chicago Black Nationalist experience. John is a man of enormous presence and intellectual power, very much the scholarly center of the doctoral program, who is as much at home teaching in a local prison as he is poring over documents in the Library of Congress. He has edited countless collections of documents both from the antebellum period of slavery and from twentieth-century political movements in the Black community. A burly man with a full beard now streaked with gray, John was the first academic in the United States to teach courses on the history of Black women, and he has just finished co-editing a large volume of materials on the relations between Blacks and Jews. John is an inexhaustible source of bibliographical references, archival information, and stories about Black scholars, most of whom he seems to have known personally. One day, after he had given a one-hour impromptu lecture in the Major Works seminar on the location of Herbert Gutman's scholarship within the entire sweep of modern historiography, I complimented him, and told him how impressive I found his command of the literature. "That's just what historians do," he replied, but I suspect there are few scholars now teaching who could have pulled that lecture out of their memory banks.

Michael Thelwell was the founding Chair of the department. Mike is a novelist and essayist, and also an expert on the Civil Rights movement, in which he played an important role. He has a special affection and respect for the work of Chinua Achebe, who is in fact the godfather of Mike's son, Chinua. Soon after joining the department, I sat in on the course Mike teaches from time to time, on Achebe's novels, and had my first sustained introduction to the literature produced by the great African writers.

One day in the fall of my first year in Afro-Am, I was a deeply moved participant in a little ceremony—there is really no other word for it—that brought closure to that awful moment fifteen years earlier when I had done my imitation of an antebellum plantation owner. Mike, whose office is catty-corner to mine across the hall, invited me in for a cup of tea. With an air of great formality, he told me about an old West African custom among the Igbo and other peoples. Young men of the same age, who together go through the rituals of passage to adulthood, form a bond of comradeship, and ever after think of one another as brothers. Boiling water on a little hot plate and carefully putting tea bags in two cups, Mike noted that he and I were of roughly the same age, and hence should think of one another as part of the same age cohort. Not a word was said of the confrontation all those years ago over the Black provost, but I knew that he was once and for all offering to forgive me, and was welcoming me into the brotherhood of those who had together created and sustained the department for a quarter of a century. We have never spoken of this, but when he reads these words, he will know how grateful I am to him for the generosity of that gesture.

Directly across the hall from me is the office of William Strickland. Bill is a political scientist and activist who ran the New England part of Jesse Jackson's campaign for the presidential nomination in 1984 and 1988. He grew up in Roxbury with Louis Farrakhan, and went to Harvard after preparing at Boston Latin. Bill is a talented polyglot who is prone to lapse into Spanish, French, or German. He has long-standing connections with scholars and political figures in Cuba, and recently took part in a ceremony in Havana celebrating the publication of the first Spanish language translation of W. E. B. Du Bois's classic work, *The Souls of Black Folk*. Bill and others worked with Vincent Harding thirty years ago to found the Institute for the Black World in Atlanta, and more recently has served as a consultant to the prize-winning television series, *Eyes on the Prize*. Although our colleagues would almost certainly dispute it, I think Bill and I are currently the politically most radical members of the department.

The last member of the group who crafted the doctoral program is Ernest Allen, Jr., currently the acting Chair. Born in Oakland, he was part of the Black Nationalist movement there and in Detroit before coming to UMass. Ernie is an expert on Black intellectual and religious movements, and has done ground-breaking work on the Nation of Islam and the various Black Masonic lodges of the nineteenth and twentieth centuries. Although he is, like the rest of us, thoroughly secular in outlook, his speech is peppered with the images and expressions of Black evangelical Christianity, and he is prone to cry "Praise the Lord! Praise the Lord!" as he walks down the hall toward the department office.

There we all were, gathered into Esther's office, arguing endlessly about which fifty books constituted the core of the field we were seeking to define. Mike argued unsuccessfully for the inclusion of at least one of Achebe's novels. Bill insisted that Gunnar Myrdahl's classic work, *An American Dilemma*, be added to the list, but John countered that it is full of mistakes and has long since been superceded. And so it went.

What was my role in this high-powered intellectual argument? The simple answer is scribe, amanuensis, and general dogsbody. If I may digress, the experience reminded me of my very first teaching job. During my stint as Instructor in General Education and Philosophy at Harvard University, I was handed the job of sharing the teaching duties in a large staff-taught history of Western Europe. As my last encounter with European history had been Mr. Wepner's class in junior year of High School, I was, to put it mildly, rather under-prepared. My colleagues in that enterprise were five brilliant young historians, for whom teaching Europe from Caesar to Napoleon was no strain whatsoever. The six of us, including such stars as Hanna Gray, later to be the Provost of Yale and the President of the University of Chicago, James Billington, currently the Librarian of Congress, and Arno Mayer, now a distinguished Princeton scholar, would gather periodically to make up lists of readings that the students could consult while writing their required essays. As the other five showed off to one another by mentioning all the latest scholarly monographs, I would nod knowingly and scribble the names as fast as I could, pretending that I was merely reminding myself of titles with which I was, of course, thoroughly familiar.

And here I was, thirty-four years later, doing exactly the same thing. As John or Mike or Bill or Esther or Ernie would mention a book, I would write it down, pretending that the title wasn't complete news to me. There were some embarrassing moments. Since it was my job to type up what we had agreed upon for our next meeting, my ignorance was on display to all. "Sinclair Drake," John gently pointed out to me, was actually "St. Clair Drake," a distinguished Black sociologist and co-author of the classic work, *Black Metropolis*. *Cane* was, of course, not written by Gene Tumor, but by Jean Toomer, *Plum Bun* by Jessie Fauset, not Jessie Faucet. And so on and on. My colleagues were endlessly tactful with this new member of the department. After a while, Bill Strickland took to drifting into my office from across the hall and asking whether I had read this or that work of Black political theory. The answer was always no [despite the fact that I featured myself something of a political theorist], and he would answer, gently, "Well, you might be interested in looking at it."

After several more meetings, we nailed down our list, and with a number of changes, it has stood the test of eight successive classes of doctoral students. Every one of the students who enter our program must start his or her education with us by reading all "fifty books" [although with successive additions and subtractions, the number has crept up to fifty-six].

Scholarly argument, activist credentials, laughter—these were my first impressions of my new department. But very quickly, I was exposed to a rather darker side of the African-American experience. Since getting official approval for a new doctoral program is a forbiddingly difficult process at the University of Massachusetts, involving review not only by a hierarchy of committees and administrators on campus but also by the President's Office, the Board of Trustees, and a state agency then called the Higher Education Coordinating Council, we decided early on that it would be prudent to consult the chief academic officer on our campus, the Provost and Vice-Chancellor for Academic Affairs. So we invited that luminary to visit with us in our offices in New Africa House.

The Provost at that time was a pleasant Political Scientist of no discernible scholarly accomplishments or intellectual distinction. He had never actually set foot in New Africa House, and over the phone displayed a certain uneasiness about venturing to what he obviously thought of as the other side of the tracks, but at last he agreed, and on July 13, 1992, at 3:30 p.m., we all sat down in Esther's office for a chat.

As soon as the meeting began, it became clear that the Provost had grave doubts about our ambitions, and it was very difficult to avoid the conclusion that he just did not think a group of Black people were capable of putting together a satisfactory proposal. "There is a great deal of paper-work," he kept emphasizing, conveying the impression that he was not entirely sure we were literate.

The rest of the department had had a lifetime of experience with the condescensions and racism of White administrators. They had long since learned to choose when to give voice to their outrage, and when to refrain in the service of some larger end. But I was accustomed to being treated with deference and respect in academic settings—one of the fringe bene-fits, I now realize, of being White. So as the Provost went on, I started to get angry.

Then, abruptly, the Provost changed his tune. Something we said— I cannot now recall what it was—suggested to him that this project might be viewed as a contribution to multi-culturalism, then becoming a popu-lar cause on our campus. So long as a doctorate in Afro-American Studies were viewed in that light, and not as a standard academic degree, he allowed as how he could see his way clear to supporting it.

I completely lost my cool. "If the Philosophy department didn't have a doctoral program, and came to you with a proposal to create one, the only thing you would ask is whether it was academically sound. But when the Afro-American Studies department comes to you with a proposal for a doctoral program, you ask whether it is a contribution to multi-culturalism. Are you saying that you hold our department to a different standard than the one you hold the Philosophy department to?"

This was 1992, and academic administrators had become accustomed to the most meticulous even-handedness and punctiliousness in any matter even remotely touching upon race. My question was little more than a rhetorical flourish. No department Chair, Dean, Provost, Chancellor—or, for that matter, Admissions Officer or Dorm Counselor—could actually admit to treating Black people any differently from anyone else, for all that they routinely did.

The Provost thought about my question for a moment, and replied, "Yes."

We looked at each other. It had become clear that we were in the presence of someone who was a greater danger to himself than he was to us. Very gently, Esther brought the conversation to a close and sent the Provost on his way. It was my first lesson in the realities of what it meant to be Black on a White campus.

In the next few weeks we drafted a full-scale proposal for a graduate program in Afro-American Studies, complete with a massive volume of attachments as specified by the documents from the administration. September rolled around, and as usual, UMass began its new academic year right after Labor Day. At the beginning of the semester, Esther called a department meeting—one of the very few formal meetings held each year.

The meeting was held in a large classroom down the hall from the department office. We sprawled in the uncomfortable chairs with their writing arms, and gossiped as Esther got the meeting started. In addition to the six of us who had drafted the doctoral program proposal, there were several other members of the department present, including Nelson Stevens and Femi Richards, a soft-spoken gracious West African scholar of African art and culture, and an expert on the design and creation of textiles.

As the meeting proceeded, Nelson, who lives in Springfield, kept getting up and looking out the window to make sure that the parking police were not ticketing his car at a metered place down below. [I try hard to resist the temptation to paranoia, but it does seem that they pay closer attention to the meters in front of New Africa House than to any other row of meters on the campus.]

Nelson's exaggerated concern triggered some comments, and then, slowly, something quite remarkable began to happen. Mike, John, Ernie, Esther and the others started telling stories about their run-ins with the Campus Police. Mike told about rescuing a stranded undergraduate one evening and being stopped by a campus policeman who saw only a Black man in a car with a White woman. Esther, who is perhaps the most widely recognized person on the entire campus, told of being called to a meeting in the Administration Building during one of the periodic racial crises, and being refused entry by a campus officer until a colleague—a White man—vouched for her. John talked about being called out in the middle of the night to speak on behalf of Black students arbitrarily rounded up by campus officers during post-game revels.

For a while, I simply listened, fascinated by stories of events so completely unlike anything I had experienced during my more than twenty years on the UMass campus. But then I grew puzzled. This group of professors had been colleagues for more than two decades. They were all natural story tellers. Surely, they had all heard these stories a hundred times. Why on earth were they rehearsing them yet again?

And then, of course, the scales fell from my eyes and I realized what was really going on. My new colleagues were telling *me* the stories, although they were apparently talking to one another. My arrival in the department had confronted them with a rather delicate problem of communal etiquette. On the one hand, I had been on the campus for twenty years, and courtesy required that I be presumed to know something of what routinely occurred there. On the other hand, I was obviously completely ignorant of what it meant to be a Black professor at the University of Massachusetts. How to initiate me into the collective experience of the department and educate me to the elements of the racial reality of the campus without unduly calling attention to my ignorance? Their exquisitely gracious and tactful solution was to engage in an orgy of storytelling in my presence, so that, like a child permitted to sit up of an evening with the grown folks, I could become a participant in the ongoing life of the community. I was deeply touched.

But that was not the end of the matter. Later on, as I thought over the stories I had heard, I realized something both startling and humbling. In two decades, I had not so much as spoken to a member of the Campus Police Force. My colleagues seemed to know many of them by name, and could tell you which ones were likely to give a Black student a fair shake. It dawned on me that they and I had been inhabiting two entirely different campuses all these years.

This is not a novel or very profound observation. At some abstract level, I had long been aware of the fact that the privileged and powerful see the world differently from those who are forced each day to deal with the insults, constraints, and worse visited on those stigmatized by race.

But this had always been for me a knowledge derived from reading or inference, not from immediate experience. Now, by the simple act of transferring from one academic department to another, I had changed the ground on which I stood, and quite literally, my *perspective* changed as well. I was a Professor of Afro-American Studies—*these* were my colleagues, not the philosophers I had left behind in Bartlett Hall. I was beginning to stand beside my colleagues, if not in their shoes, and to see the world from their place in it. That world was starting to look strikingly different.

I settled into my office on the third floor of New Africa House, and went about the usual business of being a professor, something I had done every year since 1958. Rummaging about in the drawers of the heavy old desk that I had inherited, I found several name plates, the remnants of former inhabitants. I was delighted to see that one of them read "James Baldwin." Another read "John Wideman." I was following in the footsteps of giants.

Almost immediately after changing departments, I confronted a tiny personal dilemma that, in my eyes, took on an unusual significance. Once more, some background is called for. When I joined the Afro-American Studies department, I was in my thirty-fifth year of full-time university teaching. For all of that time, I had gone through the world introducing myself, when asked, as a philosopher, or perhaps as a Professor of Philosophy. Now, philosophy has a very special cachet in our culture. It is quite possibly the most prestigious of all the Humanistic academic fields in the eyes of the general educated public. [Though not in the eyes of *everyone*, to be sure. In the army, my doctorate so impressed my basic training sergeant that he rewarded me by making me chief of the latrine cleaning squad—head head man, as it were.] Whenever I identified myself as a philosopher, I could feel, ever so slightly, a *frisson* of respect, of deference, even on occasion of awe. Oh! A *philosopher*—I could see it in their eyes, on their faces, hear it in the half-voiced acknowledgment that I was something special—not merely a professor, but a Professor of Philosophy. By 1992, I had long since become accustomed to these fleeting recognitions as somehow my due. I realize now—though not at the time—that I was indulging myself in a bit of ego-massaging each time I was called on to identify myself in a new setting. Inasmuch as there are roughly nine thousand Professors of Philosophy in the United States, there is a certain measure of misleading advertising in the announcement. Not all of us, presumably, can genuinely claim descent from Socrates. Nevertheless, I had come to view those moments as one of the perks of my job.

But now I was a Professor of Afro-American Studies, though I had retained my membership in the Philosophy department in order to continue directing several doctoral dissertations. How ought I to introduce myself from this point on? The very first time the question arose—I cannot now recall the circumstances—the entire array of possibilities flashed before my mind, and I recognized that I had to make a choice that was for me [though not, I think, for my new colleagues] profoundly significant. There were four possibilities: I could continue to identify myself as a Professor of Philosophy, which was at least technically true; I could identify myself as a Professor of Afro-American Studies *and* Philosophy, or perhaps, of Philosophy and Afro-American Studies; I could describe myself as a Professor of Afro-American Studies, but add some explanation, to the effect that I used to be a Professor of Philosophy; or, I could simply reply, without explanations or elaborations, "I am a Professor of Afro-American Studies."

I was not merely passing through the Afro-American Studies department. I had been invited to join the department, and to my rather conventional and old-fashioned way of thinking, that invitation was the greatest honor the faculty of a department could bestow upon me. To conceal or fudge my new identity would, I felt very keenly, be an act of betrayal to colleagues who had welcomed me into their world. At the same time, of course, I was fully aware that I could at any moment, if it suited my *amour propre*, revert to being a Professor of Philosophy and exact that small moment of respectful recognition to which I had become accustomed. Odd as it sounds coming from someone thoroughly secular, I experienced this permanent possibility as what Catholics call an occasion of sin. It was a temptation that it was important for me to put behind me.

I did not know it then, but I later learned that in enacting this private drama, I was reenacting a very important and public choice that had faced all of my colleagues a quarter of a century earlier when the department had been established. In the early days of Black Studies, the question arose again and again what the status would be of the men and women invited to teach the new discipline. The Academy lives and dies by tenure, and tenure is granted within departments. At many universities, such as Yale and Harvard, the administrators who were responding to pressure from Black students and the Black community wanted to get the protestors off their backs, but they did not really want to make a permanent commitment to something that they were unprepared to acknowledge as a genuine academic enterprise. So they hedged their bets, appointing Black historians, sociologists, and writers to visiting lectureships, short-term contracts, non-tenure track contracts, and—where these dodges were denied them—tenure track professorships jointly with some already established department. When the heat died down, the temporary, non-tenure track folk could be quietly terminated. Those in real tenure-track joint appointments would have to clear the tenure review process not only in the Black Studies department, but in their other departmental home as well, where, administrators could permit themselves to hope, the candidates would face insurmountable obstacles to approval. Finally, if all else failed, and the Black Studies faculty actually were awarded tenure, it would still be possible to close down the Black Studies department as a separate unit and farm its tenured faculty out to their second departments, where they could be absorbed and ignored.

In the late sixties, precisely these choices and options faced my colleagues, who were then young, untenured, and quite unsure how long their experiment at UMass would last. It is a testament to their wisdom and courage that, led by Mike Thelwell, without hesitation they insisted on regular non-joint tenure track appointments solely in Afro-American Studies. Indeed, there were several scholars to whom they refused the option of joint appointments, believing that it would weaken the department's position in the university. One scholar of Black literature asked for an appointment jointly with English and was told, gently, that he had to choose. He taught for many years in the UMass English department before accepting a position elsewhere. Thirty years later, it is clear to me that my colleagues made the right choice, a choice that undergirds our new and very successful doctoral program.

Having made the decision to express solidarity with my new colleagues by identifying myself solely as a Professor of Afro-American Studies, I now confronted the sharply different reception of my new self-description. A while later, my wife and I were at an elegant little luncheon given by an Amherst couple—she had been my older son's kindergarten teacher twenty years earlier. I was seated next to the host, who oversaw with considerable pretension the pouring of the three different wines that accompanied the meal. After a bit, just to make conversation, he asked me what I did. "I am a Professor of Afro-American Studies," I replied sweetly. He did a double-take worthy of Buster Keaton, stared at me intently for a long moment, and finally blurted out, "You're not Black, are you?"

I got a somewhat less amusing reaction while on a visit to Atlanta with my wife to have Thanksgiving dinner with her older son and his wife. Susan and I are accustomed to a glass of wine each evening before dinner, but her son and his wife do not drink, so we walked down the street to a local neighborhood establishment. I think it was the first time in my life that I have ever been in what could genuinely be called redneck territory. They didn't have wine, of course, so we settled for beer and bellied up to the bar. There were maybe ten people in the bar in all, including the bartender. Seated next to Susan was a middle-aged man, wearing a T-shirt with a pack of cigarettes in a rolled up sleeve that revealed a tattoo. Susan and I were not talking loudly, but we were obviously out of place, and everyone in the little place could hear us. After a bit, the man leaned over and said, "Are you Yankees?" I allowed as how I was [it was the first time I had ever been called that], and we got into a desultory conversation about the weather up north as compared with the local weather. After a pause, he asked, "What do you do?" Not really thinking, I said, "I am a Professor of Afro-American Studies."

The bar fell silent and the temperature dropped abruptly about twenty degrees. "I suppose you think they have been treated pretty badly, should be given jobs and all," he said. I didn't have to ask who "they" were. "Well," I pointed out quietly, "they built your homes, nursed your children, grew your food, and then cooked it and baked it, so I guess they have pretty well proved their abilities." He muttered something I couldn't pick up, and then said grudgingly, "Well, I suppose they work all right under direction." This from a man who didn't look to have held a steady job in some years. Susan and I finished our beer and left. When I told this story to Esther and Ernie the next Monday, they both said, with genuine concern, "Bob, don't do that again."

There were lighter moments, during which I enjoyed some of the sheer fun of being a member of the Afro-American Studies department. In October, 1993, I drove to New York City with Bill, John, Ernie, and Nelson to attend an enormous celebration at Carnegie Hall of the one hundred twenty-fifth anniversary of the birth of our patron saint, William Edward Burghardt Du Bois. [Du Bois was actually born on February 23, 1868, but the celebration was being held in October.] The event was intended as a fund-raiser organized by our colleague, Du Bois's stepson David Graham Du Bois, son of Shirley Graham. The idea was to raise a ton of money for the Du Bois Foundation, which David heads. After dinner at a small restaurant, we all walked up Seventh Avenue to Carnegie Hall. Nelson got it into his head that it was time to teach the White boy how to walk Black, so as Ernie, Bill, and John collapsed in laughter, Nelson strutted up the avenue and I followed, imitating him as best I could. [Nelson's walk is a wonder to behold, and I am not sure my highly amused colleagues would have done much better.]

When we got to Carnegie Hall, we ran into Esther, who had come down from Amherst in another car. Everyone was there. I have never seen so many well-dressed Negroes and superannuated Jews in my life. I held onto Esther's coat and tailed along as she greeted one luminary after another. One short woman rushed up, threw her arms around Esther, and gave her a big kiss before going off. "Who was that?" I asked. "Betty Shabazz," Esther said, searching the crowd for more friends. "You mean the widow of Malcolm X?" I sputtered, astonished. "Yes," she said, "Betty did a degree in the Ed School at UMass. We are old friends." As the evening wore on, I began to realize that my colleagues knew, and were known by, just about every Black man or woman who had become famous in the struggles over the past thirty years.

In the end, despite the fact that Carnegie Hall was sold out, the event lost money. The last straw was Bill Cosby, who went on so long on stage talking about his friend Herbert Aptheker that the union stage hands had to be paid overtime, which ate up the slender profits. I took that as a cautionary lesson for my own fund-raising efforts.

My friends from pre–Afro-Am days always had two questions about my new academic home. Why had I transferred from Philosophy to Afro-American Studies? And What did I do in my new department? Each question had a subtext, of course. The simple answer to the first question was that I joined the department because they asked me to. But the unexpressed assumption behind the question was that I was on some sort of good works or social welfare mission, bringing the wisdom of the ages to the benighted savages of New Africa House. The truth was a good deal simpler. As a philosopher, I have always prized intelligence, which is, after all, a philosopher's sole stock in trade. My former colleagues in Philosophy were, by and large, very smart, though in a narrow and uninteresting way. But with the noteworthy and happy exception of my old comrade-in-arms, Robert J. Ackermann, few of them were capable of carrying on a genuinely interesting conversation. Indeed, during my twenty-one years in that department, again with the exception of Bob Ackermann, I cannot recall ever learning a thing from any one of them, or hearing any of them say something that struck me as genuinely fascinating. By contrast, my new colleagues in Afro-American Studies are smart, knowledgeable, politically engaged, and interesting. Talking to them, I never have the distressing feeling that I am speaking a foreign language to someone intellectually challenged. It is not merely that I have learned from them—vastly more, I suspect, than they can ever learn from me. It is something much more fundamental: there are levels of irony and nuances of moral and political judgment in their conversation that keep me perpetually on my toes. When Mike Thelwell saw my son, Patrick (a chess Grandmaster) on television, playing and beating the first Black International Master (now Grandmaster) Maurice Ashley, he called me up and in perfectly deadpan Jamaican English, asked me why I had not instructed my son not to humiliate a brother. I had to do a good deal of verbal tap-dancing to conceal my failure to realize that he was teasing me. In later years, when I worried endlessly about how few applicants we had to our doctoral program as the deadline approached, John Bracey would say, in avuncular fashion, "Bob, stop worrying, they are out there, but they are operating on C.P.T. [Colored People's Time]." John was right, of course.

The second question also concealed a suppressed premise. Since I knew considerably less about Afro-American Studies than one of our undergraduate majors, what could I possibly teach in my new department? Well, I had a go at it. I taught an undergraduate course on the political economy of race and class, drawing on my knowledge of radical economics. I cobbled together a course on Black Philosophy, using collections of writings by such Black philosophers as Bernard Boxhill and Lucius Outlaw, and writings by African philosophers debating the existence of an authentically African philosophy. I taught in Afro-Am a seminar on Ideological Critique that I had first offered in the Philosophy department. But I knew, and my colleagues knew as well, that Black Studies is not my field of scholarly expertise.

So I undertook to handle all of the departmental chores that absorb the time and try the patience of senior professors. I took on the Chairmanship of the Personnel Committee, a time-consuming administrative task. In time, I became Graduate Program Director of the new doctoral program. I run the admissions process for that program. I am the sole fund-raiser for the department, endlessly seeking funds to support our graduate students. An ethnic allusion will perhaps make clear just how my role in the department evolved. In the shtetls of Eastern Europe in the nineteenth century, the orthodox Jews faced a problem imposed upon them by the rigor of the Talmudic laws to which they submitted themselves. Religious law forbade them to work on the Sabbath, and "work" was interpreted so broadly that even such simple tasks as lighting Sabbath candles were forbidden. So the practice arose of hiring a little Gentile boy from a nearby town to come in on Friday evening and perform these proscribed chores. This lad was called the "Shabbes goy." I became the Shabbes goy of the Afro-American Studies department.

Our doctoral program proposal was slowly ascending the administrative ladder, though not nearly fast enough to satisfy me. There were hitches along the way. No sooner had we drafted a full-scale proposal, with multiple attachments, in conformity with the official documents sent to us by our campus administration than the Higher Education Coordinating Council promulgated an entirely new set of guidelines, designed to make the process nigh on impossible to complete satisfactorily. We dutifully recast our proposal to meet the new guidelines, and sent it on its way again. At the very first stage of campus approval, we ran aground, thanks to the racial anxieties of a professor on a Faculty Senate Standing Committee whose job it was to recruit a three-person review subcommittee from the faculty as a whole. After nine months of stalling, she allowed as how she couldn't find anyone to serve because they were all afraid of saying anything negative about a proposal put forward by a group of Black people. In twenty-four hours, we rounded up three very senior unimpeachable scholars to perform the review, and the proposal resumed its journey. In the first flush of excitement, at the end of the summer of 1992, with a completed proposal in hand, I rashly predicted that we would surely complete the approval process in time to launch the program in the fall of 1995. This was not merely misplaced optimism. I was at that point fifty-eight years old, and I was beginning to worry that I would not be around to see the first class of students get their degrees. But nothing can be done that quickly on a university campus. Even getting approval to offer a new course usually takes an entire year. So 1992–93 passed, and 1993–94, and 1994–95 began. Finally, the proposal made its way to the office of the President, then to the Trustees, and on a triumphant day in October, was approved by the Higher Education Coordinating Council. We would have our doctoral program, after all. I mailed out a host of the eighteen thousand new brochures I had designed and ordered, and we were officially launched. The next spring, we selected seven promising applicants from the twenty-nine who applied, and sat back to await their arrival.

Meanwhile, I put my feet up on the sofa, took John Hope Franklin down from the teetering pile, and at the age of sixty-two, began my reeducation.

2

MR. SHAPIRO'S WEDDING SUIT

Stories. Since I am a New York Jew, I will begin with a New York Jewish story. Like Portnoy—whom I in no way resemble—I will make it a joke. The joke is only mildly funny, although I remind you that the standards of humor in the Academy are not terribly high. But as we go on, we shall see that this joke has deeper meanings than might at first appear.

Sam Shapiro's daughter comes home from college at the end of her junior year and announces at the dinner table that she is to be married in two weeks time. Mrs. Shapiro goes into panic overdrive and starts to plan a modest wedding for three hundred. Her last words to Mr. Shapiro, before taking over the den as headquarters for the planning operation, are "You are going to need a new suit."

Mr. Shapiro sighs, and goes to see Schneider the Tailor.

"Schneider, I need a new suit, and there's no time for fittings. My daughter, Tiffany, is getting married in two weeks time. It's got to be a real fancy suit."

"Mazel tov! Not to worry. I will make you such a suit, your own relatives won't know you."

Schneider measures Mr. Shapiro up one side and down the other, all the while assuring him that there is nothing to worry about. "Just come back the morning of the wedding," he tells Mr. Shapiro, "wearing your good shirt, your good underwear, and your good shoes. The suit will look like it was born on you."

Two weeks later, not having spoken more than ten words to Mrs. Shapiro or Tiffany in the interim, Mr. Shapiro goes back to Schneider the Tailor, with his shirt, his shoes, and underwear all just waiting to be graced by the perfect suit. Schneider whisks out the suit with an air of triumph, and tells Mr. Shapiro to try it on.

Mr. Shapiro slips on the trousers, and his face falls. The pants are a disaster. The right leg is three inches too long, and slops over his shoe. The left leg is four inches too short, revealing a quite unappealing ankle. And the waist is too big, so that the pants sag dangerously low on the Shapiro midsection. Mr. Shapiro lets out a cry of anguish, and turns on Schneider. "Schneider, you idiot!" he yells. "What have you done?"

"Now, now" Schneider croons, "don't worry. Just extend your right leg to make it a bit longer. Now hike up your left hip, so that the leg pulls up. And if you will remember to keep your stomach pushed out, the pants fit perfectly."

Mr. Shapiro is beside himself, but the wedding is in one hour, and there is nothing for it but to make the best of a bad situation. He extends and hikes and pushes, and the pants more or less cover his lower half without falling down.

Now Mr. Shapiro slips on the jacket, and this is an even worse disaster, if that can be imagined. One sleeve is too long, the other is too short, and there is a bunch of cloth over his right shoulder blade that has no discoverable function at all. Schneider the Tailor guides him through another series of contortions—one arm down, the other arm up, the shoulder hiked to fill the extra cloth, and finally, clammy with anxiety, Mr. Shapiro steps into the sunlight and makes his way carefully down the street toward Temple Beth Israel.

As he walks, concentrating fiercely on his left leg, his right leg, his left arm, his right arm, his stomach, and his shoulder, a nicely dressed stranger approaches him on the street and says, "Excuse me, but could you tell me the name of your tailor?"

"My tailor! My tailor!" shouts Mr. Shapiro. "Why do you want to know the name of that scoundrel?"

"Well," says the stranger, "I figure any tailor who can cut a suit to fit a man shaped like you must be a genius with the needle!"

We all know how the story ends. Mr. Shapiro goes to the wedding looking marginally presentable, but after two glasses of champagne, he relaxes, and his body resumes its normal shape, whereupon it becomes obvious to everyone how badly the suit fits. Mr. Shapiro can never wear the suit again. No amount of alteration will ever make it fit properly. The only thing to do is to give it to Good Will, take a tax deduction, and, of course, have another tailor cut him an entirely new suit.

Mr. Shapiro is America. His new suit—Schneider's folly—is the story White people have been telling about this country for the past four centuries. In recent times, textbooks have tinkered with the story, pushing a leg out here, hunching up a shoulder there, trying to make the story fit the facts of the American experience, but the suit never really fits, and as soon as they relax, we can all see how ill-fitting a story it is. The only thing to do, at long last, is to give the story to charity and write a new one that really fits the facts.

Let us take a look at the story of America as it comes fresh from the cutting room. This is the story I learned as a boy, like countless boys and girls before me. Indeed, until very recently, the story was still being told to college students. After we have told the old story in all its simplistic and patriotic naïveté, we will look at some of the adjustments that storytellers have made in an attempt to make the story fit the facts. Despite the efforts of several generations of alterations, even now, when we all know that the story doesn't fit, it is still being told in public by widely acclaimed and respected storytellers. Although I am no tailor, in the next chapter I will take a stab at cutting a new suit for Uncle Sam.

Rather than tell the story of America in my words alone, I shall trace its unfolding in three of the most successful American history textbooks of the past seventy years: *America: The Story of a Free People* by Allan Nevins and Henry Steele Commager, *The Growth of the American Republic* by Samuel Eliot Morison and Henry Steele Commager, and *The American Pageant* by Thomas A. Bailey.

I have chosen to focus attention on the texts written by these authors because each man was, for many years, a major presence in the American historical profession. Their books went through many editions and revisions, and served to introduce generations of students to the American story. Older readers will no doubt recognize the names of Morison, Commager, and Nevins—though they may not know Thomas Bailey—but long experience in the classroom has taught me that names, dates, and places familiar to those of my generation do not always spring readily to the minds of those fortunate enough to be younger.

Samuel Eliot Morison—"Admiral Morison" as he was known—was born in Boston in 1887 and died there eighty-nine years later. Morison served in both World Wars, as a young man in the Infantry, later on in the Navy. He was educated at Harvard, where he taught for half a century, ending his career as Jonathan Trumbull Professor of American History. I never studied with Morison during my undergraduate days, but I remember him as one of the grand old men of the Harvard faculty, a legendary figure. Morison won the Pulitzer Prize and the Bancroft Prize, both twice. He won innumerable medals, prizes, and awards, and served as President of the American Historical Association, the American Antiquarian Society, and the Colonial Society of Massachusetts.

Henry Steele Commager was born in 1902 and lived to the age of ninety-six. He taught at NYU and Columbia for many years before joining the Amherst College faculty in 1956. He was the author or editor of well over fifty books, most of them on American history. Commager was a tireless defender of liberty, a champion of Jeffersonian democracy, a fierce opponent of tyranny, whether Congressional or popular. I knew him in his last years as a puckish leprechaun of a man who, even as he approached his ninetieth birthday, retained a sharp and witty tongue and a keen eye for the manifold ways in which our political leaders fall short of the American ideal.

Allan Nevins was born in 1890 and died in 1971. [Historiography does seem to be a formula for long life.] Although he never took a doctorate, he taught for thirty years at Columbia, won the Pulitzer Prize twice, and was elected to the presidencies of the American Historical Association, the Society of American Historians, and the American Academy of Arts and Letters. Nevins was the author of fifty books and the editor of one hundred more, the winner of many prizes and medals, universally hailed as one of the leading American historians of the twentieth century.

Short of an assemblage of Nobel Prize physicists or Murderer's Row of the old Yankees, it is difficult to imagine a more formidable lineup than these three. What Morison, Commager, and Nevins saw fit to present in their texts as the American story can, I think, be taken as *the* authoritative version of that story for much of the twentieth century.

Thomas A. Bailey does not quite stand as tall as this trio, but he was a distinguished scholar whose text can be taken as representative of a great many successful American history textbooks. Born in 1903, Professor Bailey taught history for nearly forty years at Stanford University, his alma mater. He was primarily a diplomatic historian, and served as President of both the Organization of American Historians and the Society for Historians of American Foreign Relations. *The American Pageant* first appeared in 1956, and quickly established itself as an extremely successful text for both college and advanced secondary American History courses. In 1979 the sixth edition appeared with Bailey's Stanford colleague, David Kennedy, now listed as co-author. After Bailey's death in 1983, new editions of the work came out regularly bearing both his name and Kennedy's. The eleventh edition, published in 1998, was completely revised by Kennedy and a new author, Lizabeth Cohen, a member of the Harvard History department. Bailey's name still appears on the cover, but like a joint stock limited liability corporation, the book itself seems to have achieved a certain immortality.

America: The Story of a Free People, by Nevins and Commager, appeared originally in 1942, and went through several revisions, the last of which appeared thirty-four years later in 1976, five years after Allan Nevins' death. *The Growth of the American Republic* was first published in 1930. Half a century later, the seventh edition came out, now bearing the name of William Leuchtenberg, a younger historian of great distinction, in addition to those of Commager and the recently deceased Morison.

The story of America, as these historians tell it, is an elegiac triumphalist story of a free people who realize their dream of liberty by establishing for the first time in human history a body politic dedicated to the principle that all men are created equal. Nevins and Commager write:

> America emerged out of obscurity into history only some four centuries ago. . . . It is the newest of the great nations, yet it is in many respects the most interesting. . . . It is interesting because, from its earliest beginnings, its people have been conscious of a peculiar destiny, because upon it have been fastened the hopes and aspirations of the human race, and because it has not failed to fulfil that destiny or to justify those hopes. . . . America [has become] the most ambitious experiment ever undertaken in the intermingling of peoples, in religious toleration, social equality, economic opportunity, and political democracy. . . . [T]o a generation engaged in a mighty struggle for liberty and democracy [the book was published in 1942] there is something exhilarating in the story of the tenacious exaltation of liberty and the steady growth of democracy in the history of America.

As the story goes, small bands of men and women fled the tyrannical rule of English monarchs to seek religious liberty in a new world. In their native land, they had been hounded, jailed, even burned at the stake for worshipping in the wrong manner. And so they set out across a broad and dangerous sea to find a wilderness where they could set down roots, carve communities for themselves out of the virgin forests, and live freely.

In the Old World, they were trapped in a constricting network of oppressive institutions that defined their lives and dictated their futures. Every acre of land had long since been claimed, every forest and stream entailed to some hereditary ruler. But in the New World that lay waiting for them across the sea, there was a limitless expanse of virgin land that was theirs if they were willing to do the hard work of taming it and transforming it into a paradise. Save for a scattering of savages who were easily displaced, the land lay open to these intrepid seekers after freedom.

As Thomas Bailey says in the opening pages of his text:

> The American republic, which is still relatively young, was from the outset singularly favored. It started from scratch on a vast and virgin continent, which was so sparsely peopled by Indians that they could be eliminated or pushed aside. Such a magnificent opportunity for a great democratic experiment may never come again.

If freedom is the theme of our story, the central analytical idea is *Exceptionalism*. This idea, first given expression by Alexis de Tocqueville, has served as the guiding thread of both scholarly explications and patriotic invocations for more than a century and a half. America is the exception to the generalizations of historians, political scientists, and sociologists, to the time-tested laws of historical evolution defining and constraining men and women and nations in the Old World. *America is unique.* There has never been anywhere like America, and there never will be again.

Unlike all other nations that have ever existed, America is founded upon an Idea, the Idea of Freedom. There is no Idea that Great Britain embodies, even though the British, in Magna Carta, in their Common Law, and in their Parliament, have traditions of liberty. *Liberté, Égalité, Fraternité* was the great war cry of the French Revolution, but France itself was not founded on these ideals. Rome, Russia, China, Italy—none is the actual embodiment of an Idea consciously embraced by a noble band of Founding Fathers. Even ancient Greece, celebrated among Western intellectuals as the birthplace of democracy, loses its origins in the mists of legend. Only America actually embodies an Idea.

Thus, everything that happens in America is to be measured and understood in relation to that Idea. When we Americans succeed in making actual some degree of liberty, then we are fulfilling our founding Idea. When we fail for a time to accord that liberty to everyone, then we must understand ourselves as having not yet completely realized our Idea. Because an Idea lies at the heart of the American Experiment, America promises what no other nation can—the achievement of an ideal society that can serve as a model and a hope for all humanity. It is in this vein that John Winthrop wrote in 1630, while still on the Atlantic aboard the Arabella: *For we must consider that we shall be as a city upon a hill. The eyes of all people are upon us.*

America is the Great Exception in other ways as well. Alone among all the great nations of the world, America was established in an empty land, a land without the constrictions and constraints of immemorial custom. Save for those few savages so easily displaced or eliminated, the New World stood waiting for the Colonists exactly as God had created it. For just this one time in human history, a community of men and women found themselves in a true state of nature, able to build a republic of liberty and equality that bid fair to realize their cherished ideals. Thanks to the bountifulness of Providence and the vast emptiness of the North American continent, this availability of untouched land continued to define the American experience well into the nineteenth century. First the fertile Atlantic coastline, then the forests inland, then the great Western plains, and finally the lush valleys beyond the Rocky Mountains stood waiting for brave, adventuresome settlers ready to build a nation by the sweat of their brows.

And finally, because America was "started from scratch," as Bailey says, it had no hereditary rulers, no class system, no lords and peasants, no First, Second, and Third Estates. From the outset, American society has been a society of equals, free of the inherited resentments and badges of inferiority that divided the nations of the Old World. No American has been forced to bend his knee or doff his cap to the lord of the manor. Any American, no matter how modest his background or poor his beginnings, could aspire to land, to wealth, and to independence if he were willing to work hard, to save, and to seize the opportunities offered by the New World.

Samuel Eliot Morrison and Henry Steele Commager offer a literary version of this vision of America. Appealing to the work that gave the word "utopia" to the English language, they write,

> Thus, out of the welter of misery, insecurity, and corruption that were the lot of the common man in the England of 1516, came this vision of a new and better society: the American dream. One constant thread of American history has been this quest for peace, liberty, and security; this effort, often frustrated, never realized but in part, yet ever hopeful, ever renewed, to make true the Utopian dream of the blessed Thomas More.

The story of America is a fairy tale, and like many fairy tales, it begins with the invocation of an idyllic land in which magical things can happen—a fair and favorable land, balmy and welcoming to the heroes and heroines whose story we tell.

Nevins and Commager begin their book with these words:

> The history of English settlement in America began on a beautiful May morning in 1607 when three storm-beaten ships of Captain Christopher Newport anchored near the mouth of the Chesapeake Bay, sending ashore

men who found "fair meadows, and goodly tall trees, with such fresh waters as almost ravished" them to see.

The story continues as we have all learned to expect. There is the early Colonial period, the settlements at Jamestown and in what is now New England, followed by the French and Indian War and the drama of the Revolution. A good deal of space is devoted to the work of the Founding Fathers and the complex compromises that were required to form one nation out of a disparate group of independent colonies. Not surprisingly, the account tends to be celebratory. The following passage, taken from the opening pages of a twenty-five-page description by Morison and Commager of the writing and ratification of the Federal Constitution, captures the tone nicely.

> There comes a time in every revolutionary movement when the people become tired of agitation and long for peace and security. They then eliminate the radicals, trouble-makers and war-mongers, and take measures to consolidate their government, hoping to secure what has already been gained through turmoil and suffering. *Thermidor* this time is called in leftist language, from the counter-revolution in France that overthrew Robespierre and ended the reign of terror. . . . The movement that led to the Federal Constitution was essentially thermidorean in its nature. . . . Naturally it was the men of property and education whose interests were primarily affected by the menace of disunion, and who assumed leadership of the constitutional movement. But we are not to assume that it was for any exclusively selfish or class interest that they were acting. . . . Seldom has a class acted more wisely for the good of the whole, than the Federalists, the self-constituted party of property owners, publicists, and professional men that framed the Federal Constitution, procured its ratification, and built a new federal state within its frame.

The narrative continues with the story of the Jacksonian Era, expansion westward, and so forth. The details are complicated, but the story line has a certain dramatic unity. Slowly, majestically, the Idea of Freedom unfolds itself and reaches out to embrace a larger and larger fraction of the American people. The somewhat elitist tendencies of the Founding Fathers give way to the more rough-hewn frontier spirit of Andrew Jackson. Pioneers move ever westward, opening up virgin lands to civilization. Only a continent as vast as North America can offer an appropriate stage for the realization of so grand an Idea. Protected by a wide ocean from the corruption, internecine warfare, and class struggles of the Old World, America is blessed by Providence with the time and the space to fulfill its destiny as the only nation ever founded upon an Idea.

There is one small, inconvenient detail that inevitably creeps into even the most celebratory versions of the story—Slavery. Nevins and Commager record three notable events in the Virginian colony in 1619:

> One was the arrival of a ship from England with ninety "young maidens" who were to be given as wives to those settlers who would pay 120 lb. of tobacco for their transportation. This cargo was so joyously welcomed that others like it were soon sent over. Equally important was the initiation of representative government in America. On 30 July, in that Jamestown church where John Rolfe several years earlier had cemented a temporary peace with the Indians by marrying Pocahontas, met the first legislative assembly on the continent: a governor, six councillors, and two burgesses each from ten plantation. The third significant event of the year was the arrival in August of a Dutch ship with Negro slaves, of whom it sold twenty to the settlers.

Thomas Bailey records the same incident with a rather greater sensitivity to its significance.

> In 1619—a fateful date in American history—what was probably a Dutch warship appeared off Jamestown and sold some twenty Africans. Negro slavery probably would have been introduced within a few years anyhow, but this was the ill-omened beginning.

Slavery also plays a role that is difficult to ignore in the framing of the Constitution. Nevins and Commager, in their relatively abbreviated account, make no mention of it at all, even in their summary of the compromise between the small and large states in the rule governing representation in the House. Morison and Commager manage only two passing references to the institution of slavery, one of which as much as dismisses the subject.

> A careful reading of Madison's and Yates's notes on the [constitutional] debates—a luxury in which popular writers on the convention seldom indulge—reveals that slavery interested the members only as an aspect of sectional balance. [They conclude that] America was very fortunate to achieve political independence without loss of liberty, even without loss of cultural values.

Bailey offers a less enchanted picture of the process of Constitution writing. Under section headings with such titles as "Patriots or Profiteers?" and "A Bundle of Compromises," he details the deals struck by the Southern states in their effort to protect their ability to preserve slavery.

Sectional jealousy also raised its unlovely head. Should the voteless Negro slave of the Southern states count as a person in apportioning representation in the House of Representatives? The South, not wishing to be deprived of influence, said "yes." The North replied "no," arguing that the North might as logically have additional representation based on its horses. As a compromise between total representation and none at all, it was decided that a slave might count as three-fifths of a man. Hence the memorable, if somewhat illogical, "three-fifths compromise" (Art. I, Sec. II, para. 3).

Slavery was slowly phased out in the North in the first part of the nineteenth century, even as it became the very foundation of the Southern economy, though it is worth recalling that Sojourner Truth, who has become an iconic figure in the American story, was born into slavery in upstate New York and was not emancipated there until 1827.

With the entrenchment of plantation slavery in the South, and its slow demise in the North, writers from both sections began to refer to slavery as the "peculiar institution," meaning not that it was odd—quite the contrary, it was a thoroughly familiar part of American life—but simply that it was peculiar, i.e., special, to the South. It is in this way that John C. Calhoun used the phrase in his Senatorial speeches. But as time passed, the phrase took on another weightier meaning, for even to its most impassioned defenders, slavery did seem to constitute some sort of deviation from the ideals ritually proclaimed in the founding documents and rehearsed at patriotic celebrations.

As early chapters of the American story unfold majestically, all four of our authors devote so little attention to the subject of slavery in their texts that it must come as something of a shock to the unprepared reader to learn, many pages later, that a great civil war was fought over the matter. Finally however, it comes time to narrate the three episodes in the American story that simply cannot be told without some extensive discussion of the Peculiar Institution: The plantation system of the Old South, the Civil War, and Reconstruction. For a moment, the full light of the narrative shines on the Negro, before he recedes once more into the shadows, only to reappear briefly a century, and many pages, later to do his turn in the Civil Rights Movement of the 1960s. How our authors render the great events of the middle of the nineteenth century will tell us a good deal about the cut of the old story, and how it fits Uncle Sam.

The old cliché has it that the victors get to write the history, guaranteeing that their side of the conflict will be painted in the rosiest hues, but in an odd reversal of this rule with the most fateful consequences for America's understanding of its past, the South, having lost the Civil War, won hands down the struggle for control of the narrative voice of the American story.

The Planter School of American History, as it came to be known, told a story of lovely belles and courtly gentlemen, caring in their thoughtful paternal manner for charming, happy, carefree darkies unable to look after themselves and fiercely loyal to ole Massa. When the heartless, intrusive, rapacious North sought to destroy this gentle, time-honored civilization, men of honor took up their swords and rode off to defend the South, blessed as they left by their weeping wives and sorrowful Black retainers. Overwhelmed by superior forces but never defeated in spirit, the South was raped and pillaged by the Northern conquerors, who then wantonly and unthinkingly set free four million ignorant, unskilled, childlike Negroes to fend for themselves.

Worse even than the destruction of its gracious houses and fruitful plantations was the despoiling of the South's great traditions of democracy. Jumped-up illiterate former slaves, a few weeks from the cotton fields, were tricked out in stolen finery by the Northern conquerors and told to call themselves Representative or Senator. Deprived of the guidance of their former masters, these caricatures, more to be pitied than reviled, made a mockery of the halls of government in which, for generations, educated and refined gentlemen had practiced the difficult arts of self-government. Driven half-wild by the thoughtless despoiling of everything beautiful, cultured, and genteel, a few Southerners even resorted, out of necessity, to extra-legal means of reestablishing some semblance of civilization, forming such well-meaning but in the end unhelpful organizations as the Ku Klux Klan.

The Planter Historians themselves have for the most part been forgotten, but their vision of the Old South lives on in such films as *Birth of a Nation* and *Gone with the Wind*. Their narrative of these central episodes in the American story was accepted as canonical for a century and a half, and lingers even now, as we shall see, in unexpected quarters.

Morison and Commager begin the story of plantation slavery in an upbeat fashion. In a chapter called "The Cotton Kingdom," after several informative pages devoted to the economics of cotton production and the physical layout of a typical plantation, they turn to "The Slave."

> As for Sambo, whose wrongs moved the abolitionists to wrath and tears, there is some reason to believe that he suffered less than any other class in the South from its "peculiar institution." The majority of slaves were adequately

fed, well cared for, and apparently happy. Competent observers reported that they performed less labor than the hired man of the Northern states. Their physical wants were better supplied than those of thousands of Northern laborers, English operatives, and Irish peasants; their liberty was not much less than that enjoyed by the North of England "hinds" or the Finnish *torpare*. Although brought to America by force, the incurably optimistic negro soon became attached to the country, and devoted to his "white folks." Slave insurrections were planned—usually by the free negroes—but invariably betrayed by some faithful darky; and trained obedience kept the slaves faithful throughout the Civil War.

Our authors assure us that "Topsy and Tom Sawyer's nigger Jim were nearer to the average childlike, improvident, humorous, prevaricating, and superstitious negro than the unctuous Uncle Tom," although they readily acknowledge that American slavery "offered no legal escape to the talented or intellectual slave," such as Frederick Douglass.

Morison and Commager paint a heart-warming portrait of the social relations between master and slave in the Old South.

> While the average Englishman or American disliked the negro as negro, Southern slave-owners understood him as slave; Southern gentlemen still love him "in his place." There was no physical repulsion from color in the South. White children were suckled by black mammies, and played promiscuously with the pickaninnies.

There was, of course, a darker side to slavery, which Morison and Commager acknowledge.

> Flogging with the rawhide or blacksnake whip was the usual method of punishing slaves. Imprisonment lost the master their time, and short rations their health. Although the law forbade cruelty, a master or overseer was not often brought to book for it, since a negro's testimony was not received against a white man; and the abolition agitation created a feeling in the South that the white man must always be right. . . . The feature of slavery that most appealed to human sympathy was the separation of families at private sale or auction.

Despite these admittedly unfortunate aspects of slavery, Morison and Commager conclude their three-page discussion of The Slave with the judgment that, taking all in all, slavery was a good thing.

> If we overlook the original sin of the slave trade, there was much to be said for slavery as a transitional status between barbarism and civilization. The

negro learned his master's language, and accepted in some degree his moral and religious standards. In return he contributed much besides his labor—music and humor for instance—to American civilization.

When Commager and Nevins join forces in *America: The Story of a Free People*, they present a view of slavery that is subtly, but importantly, different. In a chapter titled "The Sectional Struggle," they choose as their general characterization of plantation slavery an account given by Frederick Law Olmstead in 1854. Olmstead describes a Southern plantation he had seen on his travels, what Nevins and Commager describe as "one of the first-rate cotton plantations in Mississippi." It is a benign picture of a flourishing operation on which 135 well-fed slaves labor in the fields and the big house.

> Every Christmas molasses, coffee, tobacco, and calico were generously distributed. . . . A black driver walked about among the field hands, urging them on, cracking his whip, and sometimes letting the lash fall slightly on their shoulders. . . . This was a typical plantation of the better sort.

Nevins and Commager observe that there were plantations where slavery was harsher, and also plantations where it was less harsh. But to focus either on the economics of slavery or its relative brutality, they suggest, is actually to misunderstand the institution completely. Indeed, they claim that

> few Americans, North or South, really understood the nature of the peculiar institution which one side was so bitterly attacking, the other so passionately defending.

The "most important fact" about slavery, they say, is that it was about race, not economics. "The whole institution was designed largely to regulate the relationships of black and white rather than of master and slave" so that the abolition of slavery changed little in the relations between the races. They conclude that most Southerners, who understood these matters "instinctively rather than intellectually," were "unable to explain that slavery was a transitional stage in the evolution of race relationships."

Thomas Bailey presents from the first a much darker picture of slavery. "The moonlight-and-magnolia tradition concealed much that was worrisome, distasteful, and sordid," he begins, focusing first on the drawbacks to White Southerners of their excessive dependency on the cash crop of cotton, but moving on to unflinching descriptions of the brutality of slavery. He provides a very useful analysis of the pyramidal social structure of the Old South, with a million Whites living in families with five or more slaves, another million in families owning fewer than five slaves, more than six million non-slave-owning Whites, a quarter of a million free Blacks, and four million slaves.

> The Negroes were originally seized from darkest Africa by slave traders, who crammed them into the holds of slave ships. . . . Some of the slave ships became so filthy that, with the wind in the right direction, they could be smelled before they were sighted. The death rate on the horrible "middle passage" was incredibly high, but so were the profits, which sometimes ran to 500%.

In a section ambiguously titled "The Blessings (?) of Slavery," Bailey retails the Southern justifications of the institution, taking care to impute to the Southern slave owners the views to which Morison and Commager lend the *imprimatur* of their authorial voice.

> The dusky African, *argued his masters*, was lifted from voodooistic savagery and clothed with the blessings of civilization. . . . The "fortunate" slave— *fortunate in Southern eyes*—was also fed, sheltered, and clothed, from cradle to grave. On many plantations of the Old South, especially in Virginia and Maryland, he was virtually a part of the planter's family. . . . Southern whites were quick to contrast the "happy" lot of their bond-slaves with that of the overworked Northern wage slaves, including sweated women and stunted children. . . . The uprooted Africans, despite the harshness of their lot, often gave evidence of contentment and even happiness. Their life under the easy-going patriarchal system of Virginia and Maryland had certain attractive features. [At this point Bailey seems to be speaking in his own voice.] White apologists argued that the Negroes in many cases had less cause for worry than their harassed owners, who, shackled to the system, deserved no little sympathy. The Southerners at heart were somewhat ashamed of slavery, which they delicately referred to as "the peculiar institution." If it was an evil, they felt that it was a necessary evil. But as it became more necessary, it seemed less and less evil [emphases mine].

Sometimes seeming to embrace and at other times distancing himself from these Southern rationalizations of slavery, Bailey leaves the reader in no doubt about his final moral judgment. He rejects the exculpatory views that are espoused by Nevins, Morison, and Commager, insisting flatly that

> [t]he black curse of Negro slavery could not be successfully white-washed, however much Southerners might idealize the singing, dancing, and banjo-strumming of the colored "Old Folks at Home." If bondage was such a

blessing, why did its victims universally pine for freedom, and why did so many take to their heels as runaways? Negro girl, when asked if her mother was dead, replied, "Yassah, massah, she is daid, but she's free."

Despite his unblinking portrayal of the evils of slavery, Bailey reserves his strongest criticism not for those who administered the institution, but instead for those who attacked it most vigorously. The last six section headings of the chapter which we have been examining tell the story:

> Reasonable Abolitionism
> Garrisonian Hotheads
> Violence Begets Violence
> The South Fights Back
> Ordeal by Battle
> Was Bloodshed Necessary?

Bailey lays the blame for the Civil War ultimately on Northern agitators and extremists who adopted an intransigent stance of absolute moral condemnation of the institution of slavery. As he tells it, abolitionist sentiment in the North grew slowly, for the most part urging a moderate, gradualist end to slavery designed to avoid "serious economic and social maladjustments." Even moderate abolitionism, he claims, could command support from no more than a tenth of the Northern population.

But then things took a distinctly unfortunate turn.

> The atmosphere of moderation was shattered in 1831, when a new and ominous blast came from the trumpet of William Lloyd Garrison, a mild-looking reformer of twenty-six. . . . The emotionally high-strung son of a drunken father who had deserted his wife, Garrison published in Boston the first issue of his militant abolitionist newspaper, *The Liberator*. This was perhaps the first paper broadside of a thirty years' verbal war, and in a sense one of the opening guns of the Civil War.

Bailey is clearly affronted by the favorable hearing that Garrison and his little band of "extreme abolitionists" have received from subsequent generations, and he devotes some of his strongest language to attempting to rectify this historical injustice.

> The extreme Garrison wing of the abolition movement did not understand the complex problems of the South—and evidently had no real desire to do so. . . . [T]hey demanded immediate abolition—without compensation. . . . The accusations of the extreme abolitionists knew no restraints. The

Southern "slavocrats," cried the Garrisonians, were brothel keepers and worse than criminals; they should not even be allowed seats in Congress. . . . The error persists that Garrison was the "voice" of the abolitionists. The truth is that he and his colleagues were only a small minority—the "lunatic fringe"—of the whole abolitionist movement. But his voice was so piercing, and his antics so spectacular, that he overshadowed and obstructed the efforts of the more level-headed anti-slave majority.

The South's increasingly adamant and in some cases even violent defense of slavery, in Bailey's view, was a response to the extremism of the Garrisonians.

Short of war [Bailey argues, in bringing his chapter to a close] the only feasible solution of America's slave problem was probably gradual emancipation, possibly with compensation. But the heat generated by the extremists on both sides [heat which, as we have seen, Bailey thinks originated in the North] helped destroy all hope of compromise. . . . The Garrisonians no doubt hastened the freeing of the slave by a number of years. But Emancipation came at the price of a civil conflict which tore apart the social and economic fabric of the South. About a million whites were to be killed or disabled before some four million slaves could be freed, under conditions that took the lives of tens of thousands of Negro soldiers and ex-slaves. . . . The bewildered Negro was caught in the middle. The sudden, overnight liberation of the slaves was in many ways a calamity for them. And freedom by no means solved the race problem.

And so we come at last to the Civil War, which is by universal agreement the pivotal moment in our collective history. No episode of the American story has stirred such passions, nor occasioned so fierce a battle for mastery of the narrative voice. One hundred forty years later, the war echoes in battles over Confederate flags and monuments to the war dead. It has spawned theme parks, holiday reenactments of battles, bumper stickers, and a vast library of historical works devoted even to the smallest details of the least significant moments of the most indecisive battles. There is no neutral way even to refer to the conflict. Civil War, the War to End Slavery, The Brothers' War, the War Between the States, the War for Southern Independence—each phrase stakes a claim and unfurls a banner.

The war is accorded differing amounts of space in our three texts. Nevins and Commager, the shortest of the three, devotes a scant seventeen pages to the conflict under the title, "The Brothers' War." Bailey gives the subject forty-two pages, and calls his chapter "The War for Southern

Independence," thereby signaling the direction of his sentiments. Morison and Commager, in a book close to one thousand pages long, devote five chapters, totaling 105 pages, to a detailed examination of the battles, the political struggles, and the social upheavals of the war.

By and large, as we would expect, the accounts are quite similar— Lincoln and Jefferson Davis, Grant and Lee, draft riots, blockades, the firing on Fort Sumter. The sad litany of bloody battles is here—Bull Run, Antietam, Fredericksburg, Chancellorsville, Gettysburg. The war was the bloodiest in America's history, costing almost 600,000 lives on both sides. Especially interesting is the very strong argument by Morison and Commager that the war was, for the South, from first to last about slavery, not Southern honor, or tariffs, or States' Rights, or Independence.

> The causes of secession [they write] as they appeared to its protagonists, were plainly expressed by the state conventions. "The people of the Northern states," declared Mississippi, "have assumed a revolutionary position toward the Southern states." "They have enticed our slaves from us," and obstructed their rendition under the fugitive slave law. They claim the right "to exclude slavery from the territories," and from any state henceforth admitted to the Union. They have "insulted and outraged our citizens when traveling among them . . . by taking their servants and liberating them." . . . On their own showing, then, the states of the lower South seceded as the result of a long series of dissatisfactions respecting the Northern attitude towards slavery. There was no mention in their manifestos or in their leaders' writings and speeches of any other cause. . . . All these "rights," "obligations," and "institutions" had reference to slavery and nothing but slavery.

Bailey is given to the retailing of affecting anecdotes—this is, apparently, one of the reasons for the great success of his text. In what might be called the Gone With the Wind tradition, he invokes the heroic sacrifice of the genteel Southern ladies in the face of economic ruin.

> To the hideous end, the South revealed magnificent resourcefulness and spirit. The women buoyed up their menfolk, many of whom had seen enough of war at first hand to be heartily sick of it. A proposal was made by a number of ladies that they cut off their long hair and sell it abroad. But the scheme was not adopted, partly because of the difficulty of exporting their tresses through the blockade.

On one point, all three texts agree, by omission if not by assertion. The war may have been *about* slavery, but it was a war fought between two groups of White men, with little or no participation by the human property at issue. In these accounts, and in the traditional American story as a whole, enslaved Africans and their descendants never figure as *historical agents*. From their first appearance in Virginia in 1619, Blacks are construed merely as the objects of the actions, desires, claims, counter-claims, moral pronouncements, ridicule, celebration, disgust, admiration, and struggle of Whites.

W. E. B. Du Bois, in his great 1935 work, *Black Reconstruction*, devotes a scathing last chapter to a detailed analysis of the Planter School and other historians whose writings for so long have defined our collective understanding of the war and its aftermath. William E. Woodward, in a 1928 book called *Meet General Grant*, is quoted by Du Bois as follows:

> The American Negroes are the only people in the history of the world, so far as I know, that ever became free without any effort on their own. . . . They had not started the war nor ended it. They twanged banjos around railroad stations, sang melodious spirituals, and believed that some Yankee would soon come along and give each of them forty acres of land and a mule.

In the descriptions of a great civil war fought, as Morison and Commager persuasively argue, over the issue of freedom for four million Black slaves, one might anticipate some account of how those slaves themselves reacted to, participated in, and even perhaps helped to shape the conflict. Yet in the more than one hundred sixty pages devoted to the war by our four authors, I can find only the following passage as an indication of the actions of the slaves:

> In 1863 Southerners began to feel the pinch of poverty, and as the war dragged on many came face to face with starvation. [The context makes it clear that the authors are referring to White Southerners.] Yet the South was an agricultural country, and the production of food rose as an increasing proportion of the cotton fields were planted with corn and wheat. There was no lack of labor, for the slaves remained loyal and at work, unless a Union army appeared in the neighborhood.

The climactic surrender at Appomattox left a host of great questions unanswered. Now that four million enslaved men and women were freed of the chains of slavery, how would they enter into the world of wage labor and agriculture? Under what terms and conditions would the rebellious states be readmitted to the Union? What would be the structure of political rule in the South? What was to be done with hundreds of thousands of former slave owners whose economic fortunes had rested on the enforced labor of their slaves? And what henceforth would be the social, economic, political, and legal relationships between Whites and Blacks?

The period of a dozen years or so in which these questions were struggled over and given some sort of answer was called then, and has been called since, "Reconstruction." No other part of the entire four-century-long story of slavery and its aftermath in America has so completely fallen under the narrative control of the defeated White Southerners. We hear the echo of this victory in all three of the texts we have been examining.

For Morison, Commager, Nevins, and Bailey, Reconstruction was an unmitigated disaster forced upon the honorable but prostrate White Southerners by fanatical, vindictive Northerners who were bent upon revenge and devoid of any just appreciation of the complete lack of preparation of the four million ex-slaves for freedom, economic self-sufficiency, or self-rule. Nevins and Commager devote only three pages to Reconstruction in their abbreviated history, but that is enough to give voice to the horror they feel three-quarters of a century after the end of the Civil War.

Every element of the process of Reconstruction evokes anger or sadness in them. Spear-headed by "the vindictive Thaddeus Stevens of Pennsylvania, the fanatical Charles Sumner, and other radical leaders," the national government compelled the Southern Whites to accept

> not only the Fourteenth Amendment, which made an elaborate attempt to assure the Negro of equal rights in everyday affairs, but the Fifteenth Amendment, which gave coloured men (practically all illiterate and nearly all densely ignorant) the ballot. Recent slaves, whose grandfathers had perhaps been African savages, who could not read a line of print, and who had spent their whole lives in the cotton-field, were given full voice in choosing public officers and making laws.

Of all the evils of Reconstruction, none so appalls them as the spectacle of Black men in the halls of government.

> These Negro and carpet-bagger governments were among the worst that have ever been known in any English-speaking land. . . . The South [which is to say, the White South] for a time was in despair. But not for long. Little by little, the self-respecting whites of the region gained the right of ruling themselves.

How did they accomplish this?

In part they did this by violence and intimidation. They set up the Ku Klux Klan, which compelled many carpet-baggers to return to the North, and frightened Negroes away from the voting-places. . . .

As we look back on the period of civil strife and turmoil between 1850 and 1877, it seems an almost unmixed tragedy. The country would have fared far more happily if, as Lincoln long hoped, the abolition of slavery could have taken place gradually, and with due compensation to the slave-holders.

Bailey shares Nevins and Commager's gloomy view of Reconstruction. In twenty-four pages titled "The Ordeal of Reconstruction," he expands on the themes they have set forth: the awful effect on White Southerners of being abruptly deprived of their comfortable existence, the tragicomic unpreparedness of the former slaves for freedom, and of course the political shambles produced by giving the suffrage to men "whose grandfathers had perhaps been African savages."

Agriculture—the economic lifeblood of the South—was almost hope-lessly crippled. Once-white cotton fields now yielded a lush harvest of green weeds. Seed was scarce, livestock had been driven off by the plun-dering Yankees, and the footloose Negro labor supply had taken to the highways and byways. Heart-rending instances were reported of white men hitching themselves to plows, while women and children gripped the handles.

While the "high-spirited Southerners" labored courageously, strug-gled manfully, or exhibited their womanly virtue, the slaves cut a poor figure indeed as newly freed men and women.

The average ex-slave, freed by the war and the 13th Amendment, was essentially a child. Life under the lash had unfortunately left him immature—socially, politically, emotionally. To turn him loose upon the cold world was like opening the door of an orphanage and telling the children they were free to go where they liked and do as they wished. One of the cruelest calamities ever to be visited upon the much-abused Negro was jerking him overnight from bondage to freedom, without any intermediate stages of preparation.

Most of the Negroes were bewildered and unsettled by their new status. A goodly number of the more faithful remained on the old plantation, still addressing their former owner as "massa." But tens of thousands blithely took off to enjoy their newly found freedom; and common expressions were "free as a bird" and "free as a fool."

Bailey sees the granting of the vote to the former slaves as a tactic by Radical Republicans, a devise for humiliating the defeated White Southerners.

> Stringent conditions were laid down for the readmission of the seceded states. The wayward sisters were required to ratify the 14th Amendment, thus giving the ex-slave full rights as a citizen. But worst of all, the Southerners were forced to guarantee in their state constitutions full suffrage for their former slaves.

So committed were they to this course of action, Bailey says, that they incorporated Negro suffrage into the Federal Constitution with the passage of the 15th Amendment in 1869, and its ratification in 1870.

Bailey has no doubts about the unwisdom of granting the vote to the freedmen.

> The sudden thrusting of the ballot into the hands of the ex-slaves, between 1867 and 1870, set the stage for stark tragedy. As might have been foreseen, it was a blunder hardly less serious than thrusting overnight freedom upon them. Wholesale liberation was perhaps unavoidable, given the feverish conditions created by war. But wholesale suffrage was avoidable, except insofar as the Radicals found it necessary for their own ends, both selfish and idealistic.

The result, Bailey tells us, was chaos. "The bewildered Negroes were utterly unprepared for their new responsibilities as citizens and voters." Democracy, he observes, "is a delicate mechanism, which requires education and information." The story of the Reconstruction era experiment in suffrage for Negroes "would be amusing were it not so pathetic and tragic."

Courageous in battle, chivalric in defeat, decent Whites in the South were finally unable to bear the destruction of the genteel society that they had created and sustained over so many generations.

> Goaded to despair, respectable Southern whites resorted to savage measures against Negro-carpetbag control. A number of secret organizations blossomed forth, the most notorious of which was the Ku Klux Klan, founded in Tennessee in 1866.

In Bailey's account, the KKK sounds like an adult version of Trick or Treat.

Besheeted night riders, their horses' hoofs muffled, would hammer on the cabin door of a politically ambitious Negro. In ghoulish tones one thirsty horseman would demand a bucket of water, pour it into a rubber attachment under pretense of drinking, smack his lips, and declare that this was the first water he had tasted since he was killed at the battle of Shiloh. If fright did not produce the desired effect, force was employed. [Bailey observes that] such tomfoolery and terror proved partially effective.

Bailey does acknowledge that things sometimes got out of hand.

Those stubborn souls who persisted in their forward ways were flogged, mutilated, or even murdered. In one Louisiana parish, in 1868, the whites in two days killed or wounded two hundred victims; a pile of twenty-five bodies was found half-buried in the woods. By such atrocious practices was the Negro "kept in its place." The Klan, whose original purposes were partly subverted, unfortunately became a refuge for numerous bandits and cutthroats. Any scoundrel could don a sheet.

Morison and Commager tell an expanded version of the same story, though their tone is more one of sadness than of anger. "The negro," they observe, "was the central figure of reconstruction in the South." Set adrift by Emancipation, the freed slaves were unable to fend for themselves, and their former masters, who had always had their best interests at heart, were forced to find new ways of looking after the four million freedmen.

Fair-minded Southerners at once addressed themselves to the problem of providing for the freedmen and adjusting them to their new circumstances. Most planters sought to keep their former slaves as hired help or as tenant farmers, or on a share-crop system, but the newly emancipated negro did not take kindly to labor during the first year of his freedom. Reason and persuasion failing, the Southern States attempted to deal with the situation by a series of laws collectively known as "black codes," which embodied the Southern solution to the negro problem. These black codes provided for relationships between the whites and blacks in harmony with realities rather than abstract theory.

Like Bailey, Morison and Commager have nothing but disdain for the Radical Republicans who fought in the Congress for a total transformation of the condition of the former slaves. They describe Thaddeus Stevens as "one of the most unpleasant characters in American history. . . . A harsh, sombre, friendless old man of seventy-four, and with no redeeming spark of magnanimity, he was moved less by sympathy for the negro than by cold hatred of the Southern gentry." Charles Sumner is treated no less harshly. "Vain, over-educated, and irritable, Sumner could be influenced only by flattery. He was a "complete doctrinaire," a "Yankee Brissot." [Brissot was a French revolutionary leader of the Girondin faction, who was eventually guillotined.]

Again like Bailey, Morison and Commager portray the Ku Klux Klan as brought into existence by the need White Southerners faced to "police unruly and criminal negroes in the country districts, and [to] deliver spectral warnings against the use of the ballot."

Their summary evaluation of the state and local governments in which Black legislators sat is unforgiving: "The resulting state administrations offered the most grotesque travesty on representative government that has ever existed in an English-speaking country."

With the Civil War ended and the period of Reconstruction condemned as a national disaster, Bailey, Morison, Nevins, and Commager turn their attention away from the Negro. Morison, Nevins, and Commager say virtually nothing about Black Americans after 1877. Bailey, the first edition of whose text takes us up to the Presidency of Dwight Eisenhower, offers this description of the Supreme Court's decision in Brown vs. Board of Education in May of 1954.

> The historic decision of the Supreme Court was widely hailed as the greatest victory for the Negro since Emancipation. An intermingling of the races had already occurred with unexpected success in the armed services. Now destined for the schools, it would lift from the Negroes the psychological blight of being set apart as creatures inferior. The United States could henceforth hold its head up more proudly as the Land of the Free, and give the lie to Communist agitators who insisted that America was committed to holding the Negro perpetually in the ditch.

And there it is. The American Story, with special attention to its treatment of enslaved Africans and their descendants, as told by four of America's most distinguished historians. This is the narrative suit of clothes they fashioned for Uncle Sam. It is a story of liberty, of the triumph of courage and statesmanship over natural obstacles, of occasional foreign threats, and—dominating the middle portion of the story—the great challenge of holding together a large and growing nation through the horror of a Brothers' War, a War for Southern Independence. The Negro figures only as a problem, a provocation, the occasion of fanatical abolitionist rhetoric, and eventually as the valuable property over which the great conflict was fought.

It is a great story, a moving story, a story that has proved capable of inspiring generations of patriotic White Americans. But it has a fatal flaw: it is not true. It omits or distorts a great deal that is central to the reality of American experience.

As each of the texts we have been looking at went through successive editions, all four authors took the opportunity to adjust their story to make it more gracefully fit the facts. From this distance, we cannot tell whether their adjustments, emendations, and rewritings were prompted by scholarly reconsideration or merely by the uncomfortable realization that certain things one could get away with saying in 1930 or 1942 or 1956 were simply unacceptable in 1961 or 1966 or 1985.

Some of the changes are charming or rather odd. In the first edition of *America: The Story of a Free People*, Nevins and Commager, describing the early colonies, write:

> While Virginia was thus shooting into vigor, a congregation of English Calvinists who had settled in Holland were making plans to remove to the New World.

In the third edition, this has become:

> "While Virginia was thus painfully managing to survive and grow, a congregation of English Calvinists. . . ."

Whatever the authors had learned about Virginia between 1942 and 1966, it apparently did not require an alteration of the syntax of sentence, merely the revision of a portion of a subordinate clause.

Bailey begins his story, let us recall (p. 35), with an elegiac invocation of an empty continent, whose scattered inhabitants can easily be pushed aside to make way for a great democratic experiment. That is a bit raw for Kennedy and Cohen in the Eleventh Edition, but with a few words snipped here, a few more inserted there, they are content.

> The American Republic, which is still relatively young when compared with the Old World, was from the outset uniquely favored. It started from scratch on a vast and virgin continent, whose native peoples were so few and so scattered that they were easily—sometimes brutally—shouldered aside. ["Brutally" is added, but no mention of "eliminating" them—at least Bailey was honest about that.] This rare opportunity for a great social and political experiment may never come again.

Just push your right arm down a bit, Mr. Shapiro, and the sleeve will cover it.

As we might expect, all three texts add new material covering the period between the first edition and later editions. Indeed, as Bailey's editions march on every five years or so, he regularly updates the last chapters to include whatever has happened since the previous edition. Nevins and Commager add a new section entitled "The Negro and His Rights" which gives a brief but accurate account of the modern civil rights movement, including Brown v. Board of Education, the Civil Rights Act of 1957, the integration of the Little Rock public schools, and the Freedom Riders in the summer of 1961. Morison and Commager cover much the same ground in the 1961 edition of their text under the heading "Desegregation and Civil Rights." By the time the eleventh edition of Bailey appears in 1998, much of two major chapters is devoted to the Civil Rights Movement and the modern struggle for equality, with pictures of Martin Luther King, Jr. and Malcolm X. But the greatest changes occur in the sections devoted to plantation slavery, the Civil War, and Reconstruction.

Now, if you will push your right leg down a bit, Mr. Shapiro, so that the cuff does not droop over your shoe.

Sambo is gone, to be replaced by the famous German doctor, humanitarian, and Bach scholar Albert Schweitzer:

> The Negro, as Dr. Albert Schweitzer observed in Africa, is not lazy but casual, not sullen but merry; yet always expedient. The Negro in America accepted his slave status because he had to, and got as much fun out of life as he could, consoled by a belief in a Heaven where no color line was drawn.

This in the Fifth Edition of Morison and Commager, appearing in 1962. Indeed, the authors suggest, "owing to his capacity for hard work, in addition to his adaptive qualities and irrepressible high spirits, the Negro was a great success as a slave."

Someone must have suggested to Morison and Commager that they really couldn't say things like that, because in the very next paragraph, they take a step back. "But Negro slaves as a whole are not to be described by these sweeping generalizations."

In the first edition, you will remember, Morison and Commager ended this section with the observation that "if we overlook the original sin of the slave trade, there was much to be said for slavery as a transitional phase between barbarism and civilization." In the place of this benign evaluation of slavery, the Fifth Edition offers us a post–World War II sentiment a good deal more in keeping with the moral temper of the 1960s:

> Instances of sadistic cruelty to slaves are so numerous in the records that they cannot be dismissed as mere abolitionist propaganda. [They still cannot bring themselves simply to report the fact of brutality save in this backhand way.] No doubt these were extreme cases; no doubt the majority of masters were kind and humane [they offer no evidence of this generous historical generalization]; but should not a system be judged by the extremes that it tolerates? May we not judge Hitler's regime by the gas chambers, or Communism by its purges, forced-labor camps, and firing squads?

Now the right leg, up a bit, please, Mr. Shapiro.

By 1980, when the seventh edition of Morison and Commager appeared, Albert Schweitzer's brief appearance is terminated, and there is no mention of the Negro's irrepressible high spirits, nor are we told that the Negro was a great success as a slave. The gas chambers and the Communist purges remain.

Not quite so far, Mr. Shapiro.

A number of historical evaluations are revised, or even reversed. In the 1942 edition of Nevins and Commager, Thaddeus Stevens is vindictive, and Charles Sumner is fanatical. By 1966, Thaddeus Stevens has become an "implacable opponent of the Southern 'slavocracy'" and Charles Sumner is now an idealist. For Bailey, Stevens is vindictive in 1956, and he remains vindictive even in 1998, when Bailey, now deceased, has been replaced by Kennedy and Cohen.

Rather than rewriting slanted, misleading, or outright incorrect passages, the authors sometimes attempt to make amends by adding a paragraph or an insert. Bailey's extraordinary "trick or treat" description of the Ku Klux Klan, with its ghostly figure pretending to drink water, survives all the way into the latest edition, but Kennedy and Cohen, apparently feeling the need to achieve some balance, include on the same page a contemporary text, highlighted in the manner of modern textbooks:

> *The following excerpt is part of a heartrending appeal to Congress in 1871 by a group of Kentucky blacks:* "We believe you are not familiar with the description of the Ku Klux Klans riding nightly over the country, going from county to county, and in the county towns, spreading terror wherever they go, robbing, whipping, ravishing, and killing our people without provocation, compelling coloured people to break the ice and bathe in the chilly waters of the Kentucky River. . . ."

Just push your stomach out, Mr. Shapiro, to take up the slack in the waist.

In their first editions, Bailey, Nevins, Commager, and Morison reserved their harshest language for the entry of Black men into public life during the short-lived period of Reconstruction.

> These Negro and carpet-bagger governments were among the worst that have ever been known in any English-speaking land;

> The resulting state administrations offered the most grotesque travesty on representative government that has ever existed in an English-speaking country;

> [The spectacle] would be amusing were it not so pathetic and tragic.

By 1966, Nevins and Commager have made almost a complete reversal in their evaluation of Reconstruction. Speaking of the Reconstruction governments, made up of White and Black legislators, that controlled the Southern states for a few years, they now say:

> They were, in many cases, extravagant, incompetent, and corrupt—as were some of the Northern State governments during the Reconstruction years as well. But they carried through important reforms, and they do not deserve the obloquy that has been heaped upon them.

Indeed, they issue a belated declaration of independence from the Planter School of historiography.

> For almost a century now Southerners have interpreted the Reconstruction era as one of unmitigated ruthlessness, and have insisted that a victorious North imposed upon the stricken South a Carthaginian peace. Yet no other great rebellion of modern times was put down with so little formal punishment of the vanquished, or so few acts of retribution, and no other rebellious groups were permitted to resume their positions and their power so speedily after defeat.

The shifts in Morison and Commager come early, and continue in a delicate and nuanced fashion for half a century. It was they who stated flatly, in 1930, that the Reconstruction state governments "offered the most grotesque travesty on representative government that has ever existed in an English-speaking country." In 1937, this judgment disappears, and in its place is a more complex story that includes both good and bad elements. The authors continue to talk of corruption and maladministration, although they now include a paragraph on corrupt Northern White administrations—Boss Tweed and others—flourishing at the same time. More important, there is now a paragraph on "the constructive side of black reconstruction."

What has happened in the seven years between the first and second editions to explain this dramatically altered judgment of events that were seventy years in the past? I suppose we shall never know, but it is interesting to see that in their extensive bibliography at the end of the book, the following entry appears in the section devoted to "The Aftermath of the War:"

> There is no entirely satisfactory history of the negro in America or of the freedman during reconstruction. W. E. B. Du Bois, *Black Reconstruction* is a brilliant and provocative interpretation of the period from the negro and the economic point of view and goes far to challenge the orthodox interpretation of the rôle of the negro in reconstruction.

In 1937, Morison and Commager speak of a Radical-Republican majority in the Southern states composed of

> negroes and their white allies. These last consisted of two classes; "carpet-baggers"—Northerners who went South after the war, largely for purposes of political profit; and "scalawags"—or Southern white renegades.

By 1962, they have distanced themselves from these terms of opprobrium.

> Both . . . words are, of course, heavily loaded. The one conjures up the image of an impecunious Yankee adventurer descending on a prostrate South with a carpetbag to be stuffed full of loot; the other was a word commonly applied to runty cattle and, by implication, to the lowest breed of men. There were disreputable adventurers among the carpetbaggers, but most of them were Union veterans who had returned to the South to farm, businessmen looking for good investments, government agents who for one reason or another decided to stay on in the South, schoolteachers who thought of themselves as a kind of "peace corps" to the freedmen. As for the "scalawags" . . . these were the men who had opposed secession in the first place and were now ready to return to the old Union and to take in the Negroes as junior partners in the enterprise of restoration."

But the editorial revisions of Nevins, Morison, and Commager are as nothing compared with the complete make-over to which Thomas

Bailey's text has been subjected. The eleventh edition of *The American Pageant* is an object beautiful to behold. It is big and glossy, full of expensive four-color reproductions, well over a thousand pages long. At $75.16 [my price from Amazon.com], it is a serious investment—triangulating the categories of text, coffee table book, and art object. Many of Bailey's original words can still be found in its pages, but they are surrounded by pictures of Native Americans, stories of the culture and traditions of enslaved Africans, detailed accounts of the doings of women, and the sad tale of the internment of Japanese-Americans during World War II.

And there you are, Mr. Shapiro, all ready for the wedding. Mazel tov!

So what's all the fuss? Sambo is gone, and so is Albert Schweitzer, after a brief appearance. Savages are out, and Native Americans with their own heritage are in. Slave insurrections are now acknowledged, labor unions are no longer demonized, the contributions of women are high-lighted. W. E. B. Du Bois, Martin Luther King, and Malcolm X are given their due. The narrative voice of the Planter School no longer dominates the story of the Civil War and Reconstruction. It is enough to make Lynne Cheney weep!

With these revisions, additions, subtractions, emendations, elaborations, and adjustments, isn't the old story now a fitting suit of clothes for Uncle Sam?

Alas, no. Nevins, Morison, and Commager did their best to alter the old tale, and Kennedy and Cohen have added enough spangles and ribbons to distract the eye. It is now being told about as well as one could ever hope—in fact, I wonder what Kennedy and Cohen will find to add for the twelfth edition. Even a casual look at the textbooks now being used in high schools and colleges will reveal that Kennedy and Cohen are the norm, not the exception. It is commonplace now for textbooks to high-light the contributions of Native Americans, women, African-Americans, and Latinos. No one these days would think of describing slavery as a beneficial halfway house for African savages being prepared for citizenship and civilization. So prominent have these revisionist elements become that conservatives now complain about the slighting of America's Founding Fathers. Lynne Cheney, in several widely quoted speeches and writings, attacked the national standards worked out by a committee of historians for high school American History courses, complaining that Harriet Tubman was mentioned six times in the standards, while Ulysses S. Grant was mentioned only once.

And yet, despite these salutary changes, the underlying story remains unchanged. It is *still* the story of an exceptional, a unique, land dedicated, however imperfectly and incompletely, to the ideal of liberty and justice for all. Before, the ideal was presented as though it were the reality. Now, the ideal is contrasted with the reality, and held up as the goal, the *telos*, toward which the story of America slowly, haltingly, but inexorably moves. This is still Mr. Shapiro's wedding suit, despite the alterations, and it still doesn't fit.

One striking way to see how strongly the myth grips even the most liberated minds is to look at the latest book by one of America's most distinguished historians, Columbia's Eric Foner. Foner is the author of a number of brilliant studies, including the massive and definitive *Reconstruction*, and *Free Soil, Free Labor, Free Men: The Ideology of the Republican Party before the Civil War*. The son of a distinguished radical historian, Philip Foner, Eric Foner currently serves as President of the American Historical Association. In his career and accomplishments, he exemplifies how far the American historical profession has come since the days of Morison, Commager, and Nevins.

In 1998, Foner published *The Story of American Freedom*. Foner confirms the diagnosis I have been offering, saying, for example in his Introduction:

> freedom has provided the most popular "master narrative" for accounts of our past, from textbooks with titles like *The Land of the Free* to multi-volume accounts of the unfolding of the idea of freedom on the North American continent.

Following in the path carved out by Edmund Morgan, Foner describes the interplay between bondage and freedom in Colonial America, and the interdependence of chattel slavery and the emerging ideal of free citizenship in the young Republic:

> By 1800, indentured servitude had all but disappeared from the United States, and apprenticeship was on the wane, developments that sharpened the dichotomy between slavery and freedom, and between a northern economy relying on what would come to be called "free labor" and a South ever more heavily bound to the labor of slaves. In the process, the very meaning of the words "master" and "servant" were transformed.

And yet, despite his enormous learning, great sophistication, and total commitment to the recapturing of the truth of the American past, Foner still thinks of his narrative as the *story of American freedom*. No one could do a better job of telling that story, *but it is the wrong story*. It is the story White Americans have been telling themselves for four centuries, but it is the *wrong* story.

From the outset, this has been a story about a nation founded upon the Idea of Freedom, a nation unlike any other. It has been the story of a city upon a hill, the eyes of all people upon us. I should like to tell a different story about America—a story I learned as a Professor of Afro-American Studies from men and women who have known this story all their lives. This is not my story; it belongs to them, and to the hundreds of gifted scholars, White and Black, who have painstakingly excavated it from archives and from the collective memory of a people.

If I can tell the story as they have taught it to me, perhaps others like me will listen, and we will all begin to understand the real story of America.

3

A NEW MASTER NARRATIVE FOR AMERICA

Dramatically the Negro is the central thread of American History.
—W. E. B. Du Bois, *The Gift of Black Folk*

I am going to tell this story as though Negroes were ordinary human beings, realizing that this attitude will from the first seriously curtail my audience.
—W. E. B. Du Bois, *Black Reconstruction*

Last May, my wife went to the Pelham town plant sale, and came home with a rhododendron bush, which she asked me to help her plant in our front yard, off to the right of the driveway. I am no gardener at all, but she enlists me from time to time for digging and hauling and such like chores. So I got my shovel, and dug it into the New England dirt right where she pointed. Naturally, I hit a rock. "How about over here?" I suggested, pointing to what I hoped was a more welcoming bit of ground, but no, she wanted it right there, so I tried again. When I had mapped the edges of the rock by a series of probes, cleared away the dirt, and pried it up with my pickaxe, I was sweating, and my back—never too strong—was beginning to protest. The stone must have weighed over thirty pounds, and I dragged it gingerly a few yards away, where it would be partially hidden by some tall grass.

As I straightened up, my eye fell on the old stone wall that runs along the North-East edge of our land. It is one of those falling-down old walls that you see marching through the woods all through New England, marking the boundaries of what was, two centuries ago, working farm land. I looked at the wall, then I looked down at the rock I had just dug out of the ground with such effort, and suddenly I was struck by a very simple thought that had never before occurred to me. Every one of the hundreds upon hundreds of rocks in that old wall had been dug out of this unforgiving soil with shovel and pickaxe in exactly the same way. For the very first time, my highly educated, privileged, upper middle class mind really understood the meaning of the cliché "back-breaking labor."

Colonial America

When the English adventurers and colonists came to the Atlantic coast of what is now the United States, they were looking for gold, for jewels, and for plenty of arable land, free for the taking, on which they could grow cash crops for the European market. What they found was vast stretches of virgin forest and local inhabitants whose weaponry was inferior to their own. In the end, the local inhabitants proved conquerable, though not quite so easily as the invaders might have thought at first, but the promise of precious metals was never fulfilled, at least in the Eastern part of the Northern Hemisphere, and to extract a profit from the land they seized required enormous amounts of hard, unrelenting physical labor.

We live today in an America in which most of the very hardest physical labor has either been obviated by machinery or else exported to workers in other parts of the world, conveniently out of sight, so it is difficult for us to get an accurate sense of just how hard it was in the seventeenth century to turn virgin forest into farmland and pasture. Try to imagine what sort of job it would be to fell a large tree with hand axes and saws, and then to cut its roots and dig, pry, or drag out the stump. Even with draft animals, which were hardly in good supply in the early colonies, it is crushing work. One large field, cleared of trees and rocks, surrounded by a stone wall, and plowed for planting represented a kind and amount of labor that few people in twenty-first century America do anymore.

Humphrey Gilbert, Walter Raleigh, and the other well-born adventurers who sought to make their fortune in the New World had no intention of doing this sort of work themselves. The thought must never have crossed their minds. They needed considerable numbers of people whose labor they could command, people whom they could compel to work in order to make this new land yield a profit. Their first solution was to bring with them from England indentured servants, men and women who were bound by law to work for them for seven years, in return for ship passage and the promise that at the end of that time they would be set free. In short, the New World, like the Old, was built on *unfree labor*.

Why would an English man or woman voluntarily enter into what amounted to temporary slavery? Some of them did not do so voluntarily. They were coerced, or impressed, or offered indenture as an alternative to the gallows. But for many, even so dismal a prospect was preferable to the life that faced them in their native land. At least in this fabled New World there was the possibility that they might eventually work off their indenture and get their hands on a bit of their own land.

If the indentured servants survived the voyage to America—which many of them did not—what faced them was brutally hard work, for which they were very ill prepared. England, after all, was by the seventeenth century a thoroughly cultivated and subdued land. What virgin forests remained were forbidden to common people by law. The skills acquired there as a farmer, a woodsman, or a herder were not so easily put to use in the New World. Strange as it may seem to us now, it takes experience and skill to cut down a tree or make a field arable, and the workers frequently wounded themselves with wayward axes or broke their tools on the harsh soil.

The constant and insistent worry of the masters was how to extract from their servants the hard work that would make their investment profitable. Not surprisingly, the indentured servants frequently shirked the most painful of the work, running away, or even turning on their masters. The scanty law records tell many stories of servants who disappeared into the woods, or put down their tools once their masters were out of sight. The response of the masters was angry, frustrated, and incredibly harsh—at least by our modern standards. Whipping was commonplace, as was starvation. Servants were sometimes punished by having their ears cut off. Jacqueline Jones, in her brilliant book *American Work*, tells the story of

> Alice Travellor, the mistress of a little girl named Elizabeth Bibby, [who] showed no remorse after hoisting the girl "upp by a Tackle which they use to hang deare with," whipping her, holding her "over the fyre threatening that she would burne her," and beating her bloody. Elizabeth had enraged her mistress by soiling her bed.

Servitude was not an oddity or rarity in Colonial America. It was the norm. Most of the men, women, and children in the early colonies were unfree laborers of one sort or another. Freedom—the legal right to live where one chose, marry whom one chose, work when and in what way one chose—was the precious possession of the upper classes, and of very few others. From the very beginning, the American Story has been a story of *bondage*.

There is nothing unusual about this fact, of course. Bondage of one sort or another had for many centuries been the lot of most of the people living in Europe, and of most of the people living in Asia, for that matter. Colonists from powerful states routinely killed or enslaved the militarily less powerful inhabitants whom they encountered as they established their colonies. But that is just the point. What happened in North America was not *exceptional*, it was quite ordinary. The traditional American story is simply wrong in its two foundational themes: America was not founded as the embodiment of The Idea of Freedom, nor is it unique, exceptional, unlike all other nations. America got its beginning as simply one more collection of colonies built with forced labor.

Thus far, we have been talking only about White people, but there were others here. There were the local inhabitants, whose wishes, needless to say, had not been consulted when the colonies were planted in their midst. The colonists vacillated between trying to establish friendly relations with the locals and trying to exterminate them. On occasion, their behavior was simply self-destructive. The local inhabitants, after all, had long ago figured out how to live with reasonable comfort in the forests along the Atlantic shore of North America. Simple self-interest might have suggested that they would be a good source of advice to the perpetually hungry settlers. But a combination of ethnocentric arrogance, xenophobia, and just plain stupidity led the settlers again and again to turn their backs on even the friendliest of their new neighbors.

In the earliest days of some of the colonies, such as those in Virginia, the chances of surviving for more than a few years were very slim indeed. It seems incredible to us now, but the records clearly show that as many as eighty percent of those who came to Virginia from England in the first decades of the seventeenth century died of famine or disease or overwork within three or four years. Some were lost in battles with the Native Americans, but their numbers are as nothing compared with those who just didn't make it. Despite this fact, shiploads of indentured servants kept arriving, and eventually the settlers began to tame the land, and learn how to survive. At the same time, thanks to the insatiable demand for tobacco back in Europe, the investors on occasion made some serious profits.

The first Africans came to North America in 1619, but it was several generations before there were significant numbers of them in the colonial workforce. It seems natural to refer to that first group of twenty, and all who followed, as slaves, and they most certainly were unfree. But it would be half a century or more before the term "slave" acquired the full sense that we associate with the word.

The earliest records of the colonies reveal a considerable confusion and uncertainty about the status of the African forced laborers, as compared with that of their unfree White fellow workers. The problem—if I can put it that way—was that the traditions of the English Common Law had no concept of chattel slavery. Bondage had a long and well-established history, but the Common Law lacked the useful idea of a human being as a piece of property, having no legal rights or standing in a court, and subject to being bought and sold like a horse or a plow or perhaps—a touchy matter this—like a piece of land. From the arrival of the twenty Africans to the final, bloody termination of chattel slavery in 1865, the lawyers and the courts first of the Colonies and then of the States struggled with this conundrum.

Among the many problems posed by the Common Law was the well established rule that the legal status of the child follows that of the father. In England, a son sired by a well-born father on a scullery maid was still well-born, for all that he might have to forego his claim to a share of the paternal estate. But once chattel slavery began to develop in the New World, it occurred to the masters that they would be turning their backs on valuable property if they were to allow their bastard sons and daughters to claim the status of freemen and women. Like all legal subjects, it would seem, this matter is almost unmanageably complicated, but eventually the principle came to be established that the children of a slave mother were the property of her owner, regardless of who the father was [including the owner himself]. In the Latin of the law courts, *partus sequitur ventrum* [the issue follows the womb].

As time passed, the courts fashioned a clearer and more rigid legal status of *slave*, and sorted out the endless logical and practical problems generated by the treatment of human beings as property. But to the very end, there never was anything that could definitively be called "*the* law of slavery" in the United States.

Very early on, the lowest and least privileged status in America was reserved for the Africans and their descendants. Africans were punished more severely than Whites, they were more often consigned to permanent unfreedom, their children were bound to the status of their parents, and they were denied even the scanty protections that the law offered to White indentured servants. By the late seventeenth century, something very like full-scale chattel slavery was coming into existence in a number of colonies. The legal records contain the evidences of lawyers and judges puzzling over whether to consider slaves chattels personal—in which case they were liable to be the first property sold off to satisfy the debts of a dead man's estate—or chattels real, in which case they, like land, would be the last elements of an estate to be sold. Needless to say, the dispute had nothing to do with the feelings or rights of the slaves, who had neither in the eyes of the law. But it mattered a good deal to a widow, who might end up with land and no slaves to work it.

There are many signs in the earliest records of what we today would call racial prejudice. Nevertheless, it would be a very bad mistake to suppose that Africans were exploited, oppressed, and used as cheap labor *because* of racial prejudice. The central fact of Colonial America was unfree labor—bondage—and Africans were brought here by force from their homes for the same reason that English men and women were bound by indenture—because those who ruled the colonies had an insatiable need for forced labor. As John Bracey said to me one day when I was going on in the Major Works Seminar about racial prejudice in the early days of America, "Bob, when the English got to North America, they didn't look around and say, 'This is an ideal place, a perfect place to create a new society. We've got everything we need except some Black people to dislike. Let's go get some and bring them over here so that we can discriminate against them.' "

It sounds pretty silly when you put it that way, but John was making an important point, especially in light of the current view in some quarters that African Americans are not good workers. The Africans were kidnapped and brought here because the colonists believed they would be productive workers, despite the necessity of forcing them to that work by whippings and even mutilations. In some parts of Colonial America, Africans were preferred over other forced laborers precisely because of their special skills. In South Carolina, for example, where rich rice plantations were established along the Waccamaw River, it was the agricultural skills of West Africans that made the profitable enterprises possible.

Charles Joyner tells the story in his beautifully evocative study, *Down by The Riverside*. It is worth listening to him for a bit.

> Africans were in South Carolina from the beginning of settlement and played a major role in establishing rice culture. . . . The early technological knowledge was supplied by Africans, not Europeans. To support this statement it is not necessary to establish that all, or even most, of the Africans who came to South Carolina were experienced in rice culture. All that is

necessary is to point out that none of the Europeans, whether from the British Isles, Western Europe, or the Caribbean, had any experience with rice culture at all. . . . Rice . . . was plentiful along the entire West African coast . . . especially in the Senegal-Gambia region that supplied nearly 20 percent of the slaves imported into South Carolina.

The behavior of the White settlers toward the Native Americans differed markedly from that directed at the captured Africans who were brought to the New World and enslaved. At first, the settlers made some efforts to enslave the Native Americans as well, but the attempts were unsuccessful. In frontier conditions, it was too easy for the local inhabitants to slip away into the woods and return to their own people. Hence the settlers and their descendants adopted a policy of displacement and extermination, rather than enslavement and incorporation. Native Americans were slaughtered, and those who survived were marginalized. As a consequence, Native Americans have not played, in the American story, the central role that the Africans and their descendants have occupied.

It is instructive to contrast the experience of North America with that of Central and South America. There the local populations *were* impressed into service as forced laborers, and worked along side Africans under the rule of Whites. So the true story of what has come to be called Latin America *is* centrally and unavoidably the story of the sufferings and the actions of the native population.

Over a period of a century and a half, two parallel processes unfolded, each of which was intimately linked with the other. The first was the slow emergence, through legal rulings, acts of force, and economic choices, of the racially encoded status of chattel slave. Little by little, the unclarities and uncertainties concerning the status of the African workers and their descendants were sorted out. By the middle of the eighteenth century, it had become established in North America that Black men and women were property, to be used as a source of agricultural labor and craft labor, as house servants, and on occasion as sexual objects. So long as it was legal to import more slaves from Africa, there was little emphasis on their use as breeders of new slaves. That would come later.

Slaves could be bought at auction, sold on the open market, transferred from owner to owner in much the same manner as farm animals. Owners were free, within very broad limits, to use whatever kind and amount of force they chose to extract work from their slaves. Slaves were regularly whipped, branded, mutilated, and starved into something like submission. Slave owners were loathe to kill their slaves, since each Black man, woman, or child represented a good deal of invested capital, but if, as sometimes happened, the "chastisements" got out of hand and a slave died, it was extremely unlikely that a White man or woman would face legal action. There were exceptions, of course. If you rented the services of a slave from his owner, and in the course of "correcting" the slave maimed or killed him, then of course his owner would have a cause of action against you. The law was punctilious in its protection of property rights.

In the earliest days of the colonial period, it would appear that some White men and women were consigned to a status very like that of slavery, and from the beginning all the way to the end of slavery, there were Black men and women who were legally free. But as time went on, it became settled in practice and in law that to be a slave was to be Black and to be White was to be free.

The relegation of a substantial portion of the people in Colonial America to the category of property had some odd and troublesome consequences that persisted unresolved until 1865. Regardless of what the law might say, the slaves actually were people—sentient beings with reason, intelligence, speech, purpose, agency, and all the other marks of humanity. If one White man attacked another White man, or stole his horse, or raped his wife, it might well be that the only human witness to the deed was a slave. But as a piece of property, the slave had no legal standing, and hence could not testify in court, any more than a horse or pig or wagon could testify.

More problematic still to the slave owners, many of the slaves converted to some form of Christianity, a possibility clearly open only to a creature with an immortal soul. What was one to make of a *non-person* who was a communicant?

The slavery that evolved during the first century and a half of Colonial America was hereditary. The children of slaves were slaves, the property of the owner of their mother. This meant that there was not merely a *status* of slave that individuals occupied, but in fact an entire hereditary *caste* of slaves, condemned forever to be born into slavery, to live and die in slavery, and to pass on the curse of slavery to their descendants.

White masters regularly raped their slaves as a way of increasing their wealth, for with the closing of the slave trade in the early nineteenth century, the market price of slaves rose, and a slave baby was a valuable addition to a master's property holdings. A good deal has been made recently of the sexual relationship between Thomas Jefferson and Sally Hemmings, as though such a connection was unusual and noteworthy, but in fact, forced miscegenation was so widespread that today, a very large portion of the

White American population is actually of what was once called "mixed blood," whether they know it or not.

From time to time, slave masters who had become fond of their slaves, and had even, perhaps, cohabited with them or fathered them, freed them from the bondage of slavery, and declared them henceforth to be free men and women. [One is reminded of the Emperor Caligula, who made his horse a member of the Roman Senate.] There is something legally and logically peculiar about this process of individual *manumission*.

In America at that time, if I owned a pig, the law protected my exclusive right to the use and enjoyment of that pig. Should there come a time when I no longer wanted my pig, I had every right to turn it loose in the forest to run freely [no longer so easy, of course even in rural America, what with zoning laws and such]. I might even go so far as to publish an advertisement in the local newspaper declaring that henceforth I forswore all claim to the pig. But I clearly did not have the authority to forbid any other person from seeking out that pig and making it his or hers. I did not have the right to say to the world: "No one may seize that pig and declare ownership in it." In other words, I did not have the authority to declare that the pig was for all time *unownable*.

But that is precisely what a slave master did by freeing or manumitting a slave. When George Washington, in his last will and testament, freed his slaves [an act that somehow eluded Thomas Jefferson], he forbade anyone in the new nation from ever enslaving them again. It is a testimony to the logical absurdity of slavery that manumission was recognized and acknowledged as a legitimate act.

While full-blown chattel slavery was emerging from the early-seventeenth-century confusion of bound labor, a parallel process was taking place with regard to the status of Whites. As time passed, the condition of the White indentured servants was progressively ameliorated. Laws were passed forbidding some of the more extreme forms of abuse visited by masters on their servants. Perhaps even more important, limits were placed on the practice of renewing or extending a servant's time of indenture for even the most minor infractions or acts of rebellion.

Indentured servitude was not entirely eliminated by law until the passage of the Thirteenth Amendment to the Constitution in 1865 ["Neither slavery nor involuntary servitude, except as punishment for crime whereof the party shall have been duly convicted, shall exist within the United States, or any place subject to their jurisdiction"], but the practice slowly died out in the early nineteenth century. Little by little, rights and protections that had originally been enjoyed only by the elite few came to be the birthright of virtually all White inhabitants of the colonies.

The development of chattel slavery and free citizenship was more than merely a parallel evolution of two unconnected ideals. Each depended in complex ways on the other. Edmund Morgan first spelled out this intimate relationship a quarter of a century ago in a book that has earned the reputation of a classic among professional historians. In his study of Colonial Virginia, *American Slavery, American Freedom*, Morgan details the ways in which the transformation of indentured servants into free citizens actually prompted landowners to turn to slave labor.

> The connection between American slavery and freedom is evident at many levels if we care to see it [he observes]. As Virginians nourished an increasing contempt for blacks and Indians, they began to raise the status of lower-class whites. The two movements were complementary.

Recently, some authors have taken to using a rather uncomplimentary term for states that fit the description I have been developing of America. They call them White Settler States. For most of us, that conjures up pictures of British East Africa or Portugese Angola or perhaps the South Africa of the Boers. We White Americans don't like to see ourselves in such pictures. We much prefer Land of Freedom, Land of Liberty, a welcoming home to huddled masses yearning to be free. But facts are facts, and if the shoe fits . . .

Thus Liberty and Slavery emerged from the same inchoate mixture of unfree labor, during the more than century and a half between the settlement of the first colonies and the establishment of the United States. When it came time for the Founding Fathers to craft the Constitution, they wrote into it *both* the assurance of extensive liberties to Whites, *and* the ratification of enslavement for Blacks. The liberties of Whites were guaranteed by the republican form of government and by a group of Amendments that guaranteed to all Whites [or at least to all White males] rights, privileges, and protections that a century earlier had belonged only to an elite few. As for slavery, the Framers never used the word "slave" or its cognates. Instead they spoke of "free persons, including those bound to service for a term of years" to refer to White people, and "other persons" to refer to slaves. They thus resolved in their founding document the question whether the slaves were persons, while guaranteeing that their owners could continue to treat them as property.

The Revolutionary War was a time of excitement and great hope for the enslaved Africans and their descendants. Perhaps understandably, they allowed themselves to take seriously the rhetorical flourishes about Inalienable Rights and the creation as equal of all men. As part of the war effort, the British held out the prospect of freedom for slaves who deserted their masters and came over to the Loyalist side. In 1775, the English Governor of Virginia issued a proclamation conferring freedom on all slaves and indentured servants who came over to fight on the loyalist side. As John Hope Franklin tells the story, "Thomas Jefferson estimated that in 1778 alone more than 30,000 Virginia slaves ran away," and comparable numbers fled from slavery in South Carolina and Georgia.

In response to these losses of bound labor, the rebels adopted a more accommodating attitude toward the slaves who remained in their possession. But they were committed to slavery as a source of labor, and with their victory over the British, the Founding Fathers made sure to write slavery into their Constitution. It is interesting to speculate what might have become of Black Americans had the Crown succeeded in putting down the rebellion.

Slavery was not a quirk, an oddity, a peculiar and temporary flaw in the shining character of the Republic being born. It was the economic foundation of the wealthiest of the rebellious colonies. America, as the Framers of the Constitution conceived it and created it, was not to be The Land of Freedom. It was, in fact and in law, to be The Land of Slavery and Freedom.

Plantation Slavery

By the time the first administration of the new republic took office, the outlines had emerged of the institution of plantation slavery that would dominate the Southern half of the United States until the Civil War. The North had always been a society *with* slaves—a society, that is to say, in which some members of the labor force were legally unfree and had the status of property. The South, however, became a *slave society*—which is to say, a society whose entire economy rested upon slave labor. This is the society romanticized in fiction and in the writings of the historians who were labeled by W. E. B. Du Bois as the "Planter School." The followers of U. B. Phillips and W. A. Dunning painted a picture of gallant Southern [White] gentlemen, genteel Southern [White] ladies, and barbarous, incompetent, child-like Blacks that lingers even to the present day. The real nature of ante-bellum Southern society could from time to time be glimpsed in newspaper advertisements for runaway slaves, in the records of slave auctions, and in the slave narratives that became a popular weapon of the Northern abolitionist movement.

Some of the very best historical writing of the last quarter-century has been devoted to the subject of American slavery, and we have learned an enormous amount about every aspect of it. But we must never lose sight of one fundamental fact: from first to last, slavery existed to extract forced labor from a large and productive work force, in order to make a profit on investments in land. At first, the principal cash crops were tobacco, rice, sugar, and indigo, but the invention of the cotton gin at the end of the eighteenth century transformed the Southern economy, resulting, among other things, in a vast forced migration of slaves to the Southwest toward land more favorable to cotton production.

Most slaves in America were agricultural laborers, as were most Whites. Not until the twentieth century did the division in the national workforce between agricultural and industrial labor shift away from agriculture. But the large plantations were very much self-contained economic units, and slaves did every conceivable sort of work. Slaves worked as carpenters and as blacksmiths, as wheelwrights, wainwrights, coopers, iron smiths, and coppersmiths, as teamsters and wranglers, as butchers, bakers, wet nurses, nurse maids, butlers, scullery maids, hand maidens, and footmen, as drivers, drovers, and herdsmen. Slaves sailed ships, and they built ships. On occasion, slaves even designed the fine mansions that they built for their masters—and, we now know, in fact built the White House in Washington, D. C., itself.

It was quite common for slaves to be rented out by their masters to work on other plantations or as skilled craftsmen in nearby towns. Strange as it may seem to us today, slaves worked as industrial laborers in factories. Some factories were staffed entirely by slave labor and there are even a few cases in which enslaved Blacks, free Blacks, indentured Whites, and free Whites worked side by side in the same factory.

The first time I visited South Africa, I was driven from the Johannesburg airport along broad multi-lane highways into the city. It took me a while to realize that these highways, like most of the rest of South Africa, had been built by the labor of African workers. The same thing is true of the Old South. Those graceful mansions in which genteel ladies served tea to courtly gentlemen were all built and maintained by slaves. Whatever work needed doing on the plantations was done by slaves.

The plantations were first and foremost economic units established to generate steady profits, and the records are full of the detailed calculations by masters designed to maximize the yield from their enslaved labor. The treatment of the slaves was routinely brutal, as was the treatment of farm animals. The accepted method for getting a team of oxen to pull was to whip them, and the accepted method for getting a team of slaves to chop cotton was to whip them as well. But the inconvenient *humanity* of the slaves elicited from their masters an additional measure of sadism that cannot entirely be accounted for by the rationality of double entry bookkeeping.

The slaves, after all, were *people*, and they resented their oppression and exploitation, whose nature they understood quite well. Their constant resistance was both an affront to their masters, and a threat to them as well. The methods used by masters to cow, subdue, and dominate their slaves were hideous in their cruelty. Slaves were routinely hung up by their hands from a rafter until their feet were off the ground, and then whipped with rawhide until the blood ran freely down their bodies and soaked into the earth below. Coarse salt was then rubbed into the wounds, causing excruciating pain. Many slaves bore deep scars and welts on their body from such beatings until the day they died. Pregnant slaves were expected to continue working until they gave birth, and their resistance, like that of the men, was punished with whippings. But to whip a pregnant woman in the ordinary manner threatened the life of the unborn child, which was potentially a valuable bit of property, so on some plantations, a shallow hollow was dug into the ground, in which the woman was forced to lie face down during the beating. In that way, her foetus was protected while she was being whipped.

Needless to say, any individual slave was not likely to be whipped very often. Robert Fogel and Stanley Engerman, in a widely discussed and much criticized book, report that on one plantation whose owner, Bennet Barrow, kept careful records of his two hundred slaves, about half the slaves were not whipped at all during a two year period, and overall there were 0.7 whippings per slave per year. Since a number of readers have actually concluded from this bit of data that things weren't so bad in the Old South, I tried a little thought experiment in an effort to imagine what effect whippings might have had on a slave.

Down the road from the University of Massachusetts is Amherst College, a famous private liberal arts institution that has on several occasions been ranked the best college in America. It has a faculty of two hundred—just about as large as the slave population on Barrow's plantation. Suppose a whipping post were set up in front of the Robert Frost Library in the central college common. And suppose that on an average of once every four or five days, an Amherst College professor were stripped to the waist, man or woman, and whipped at that post until the blood ran for some infraction of college rules or simply for failing to grade papers on time. Now, as a member of the faculty, I would presumably be intelligent enough and educated enough to be able to calculate that my chances of being whipped were only 0.7 per year, and I would also have noticed that if I was extremely careful, and never talked back to the Dean or the President, I might never be whipped at all. Nevertheless, I think it is reasonable to suppose that the steady progression of brutal public whippings would have, how shall we say, a chilling effect on me.

Such a fantasy seems absurd, of course, but that is just another way of saying that we White people don't really think of the slaves as people like ourselves, regardless of the political correctness of our sentiments. Whipping slaves is terrible, cruel, inhuman, but it is something that happens to *other* people, whereas whipping professors, bizarre though that may sound, is something that might happen to *me*.

Despite their back-breaking labor and the brutality visited upon them by their owners, the slaves succeeded in capturing enough time and space for themselves on the plantations to create and sustain a considerable family, social, artistic and religious existence. Much of their culture was a continuation and transformation of the rich and complex culture of the African civilizations from which they had been kidnapped. This is evident in their language, their kin relations, their agricultural skills, their music, and even in the architecture of their homes, which in some cases can be traced to styles of West African housing. Morison and Commager actually had it about right when they described slavery as "a transitional status between barbarism and civilization." They just had the direction of the transition reversed.

From the very earliest days of the fledgling colonies, those who commanded the forced labor of others worried about resistance, rebellion, and insurrection. Mules are famously balky, but no muleskinner fears a conspiracy of his mules. Slaves, on the other hand, were constantly resisting the control of their owners. The most common resistance was passive and covert—slacking off in the field as soon as the driver turned his back, stealing a pig or burning down a sugar house, or even spitting in the master's food before serving it to him. So many slaves ran away from their owners that in many parts of the South the gentry organized mounted patrols to scour the woods and roads for runaways. The paterollers, as the slaves called them, figure in much of the folk lore of the time, and the newspapers regularly ran advertisements offering rewards for the capture and return of runaways.

With very limited knowledge of the geography beyond the local area, and no transport or support system to help them, most runaways were caught not far from their places of servitude, and returned to be punished and put back to work. Many ran away several times, sometimes simply in order to visit a wife, a husband, or a child who had been sold to a nearby plantation. Even the Underground Railroad, which has achieved legendary status in the iconography of the abolitionist movement, assisted relatively few escapees to freedom in the Northern states or Canada.

There were organized slave rebellions, most famously by Nat Turner in 1831 and Denmark Vesey a few years earlier. Despite the myths of happy slaves and caring masters, White Southerners were well aware that their human chattels were ready to rise up against them given the slightest chance, and all during the first half of the nineteenth century, the laws, the press, and the popular literature of the region throbbed with a fear of rebellion that bordered on hysteria.

And so we see that for the first two and a half centuries of its existence, America was a land of bondage and forced labor, as well as a land of democratic freedom and free labor. Bondage and freedom were so inextricably intertwined that neither can be understood without the other. Every part of the American experience was shaped and defined by the duality of freedom and bondage. The economy rested upon slave labor in the South and free labor in the North. The laws of the several states, and of the nation as a whole, were shot through with dictates, decisions, and contradictions designed to accommodate the fact of slavery. The terms of the expansion Westward, and the principal struggles of national politics, were all covertly or overtly about slavery. In the South, the grandees who owned the great plantations and controlled the public life of the society used the existence of slavery to keep in line the three-quarters of the White population who owned no slaves. This dual system of labor—slave and free—was racially encoded, and despite the slow disappearance of slavery from the Northern states, that encoding determined the fate of Whites and Blacks there as well as in the South. The Bible was appealed to as the authority for the exploitation and oppression of Black Americans, and this traditional rationale was joined by pseudo-scientific theories of race put forward by respected scientists.

It would be false to say that America was essentially a land of slavery in which there was freedom *on the side*, but it is equally false to describe America as a land of freedom that oddly, unaccountably, harbored slavery as a *peculiar institution*. Until we face honestly this persistent duality in the foundation of American economy, law, and society, we cannot even begin to understand the nation in which we now live.

In light of this duality, it is surely fitting that America's greatest trauma was a war fought between brothers and neighbors to determine whether freedom and bondage would continue to define the American experience. From the outset, the Civil War was about the continuation of slavery. It was the threat to their forced labor supply, and to the political power that flowed from the ownership of slaves, that moved the Southern states inexorably toward secession. The North was at first prepared to reestablish the Union without ending slavery, but as the war progressed, the conflict was transformed, so that it could only be ended with the total elimination of the bondage of Black Americans.

Black men and women had from their first arrival played an important part in the economic development of North America, and before the war, some of them had taken active roles in the abolitionist movement in the North. But during the Civil War, the great mass of slaves for the first time became significant actors in the great public affairs of the nation. It was W. E. B. Du Bois who first pointed this out, in his magisterial revision of American historiography, *Black Reconstruction*. Du Bois took from European radical theory the concept of a General Strike—that is to say, an economy-wide strike of workers in every industry not for immediate economic gain but as a political weapon to destroy capitalism as a system. Against the entire tendency of American historiography, Northern and Southern, he argued that the Southern slaves withheld their labor from their owners, and by the tens of thousands defected to the Union armies, thereby crippling the Southern war effort and finally bringing about the defeat of the South. In this paragraph, taken from Chapter 4, "The General Strike," he gives us the core of his thesis:

> It must be borne in mind that nine-tenths of the four million black slaves could neither read nor write, and that the overwhelming majority of them were isolated on country plantations. Any mass movement under such circumstances must materialize slowly and painfully. What the Negro did was to wait, look and listen and try to see where his interest lay. There was no use in seeking refuge in an army which was not an army of freedom; and there was no sense in revolting against armed masters who were conquering the world. As soon, however, as it became clear that the Union armies would not or could not return fugitive slaves, and that the masters with all their fume and fury were uncertain of victory, the slave entered upon a general strike against slavery by the same methods that he had used during the period of the fugitive slave. He ran away to the first place of safety and offered his services to the Federal Army. So that in this way it was really true that he served his former master and served the emancipating army; and it was also true that this withdrawal and bestowal of his labor decided the war.

When Du Bois wrote this passage in 1935, he was a voice crying in the wilderness. Not only the Planter School, but, as we have seen, the leading Northern American historians as well, completely rejected such a view of the role of the slaves in the Civil War. It took the Historical profession half a century to catch up with him, but in the end, it turns out that he was right.

In the 1980s, a massive research project was undertaken by a group of scholars at the University of Maryland, involving an examination of two million Civil War documents in the National Archives. [When I first read about this project, I did a little back-of-the-envelope calculation, and concluded that it would take someone twenty years, working two thousand hours a year, looking at a document a minute, allowing ten minutes an hour for bathroom breaks, to actually look at two million documents!] Using the labor of untold battalions of graduate students, and drawing on materials that Du Bois could never have had access to, Ira Berlin, Barbara Fields, and others demonstrated that the actions of the slaves did indeed change the nature of the war and make a critical difference in its outcome. The arrival in the camps of the Northern armies of a ceaseless flow of "contraband," as the runaway slaves were called, forced the generals and the politicians to make a series of fateful decisions.

Legally, these men, women, and children were the property of their masters, and a due regard for property rights required that they be returned to the plantations from which they had fled. But these were the workers whose agricultural and other labor was producing the war materiel the South needed to prosecute the war. To return them would work directly against the military interests of the Northern armies. What is more, the runaway slaves offered to provide much-needed labor in the army camps, and even to take up arms and swell the always undermanned ranks of Northern regiments.

In the process of offering protection to the runaways and enlisting their services in the war effort, the North found its war aims transformed. Slowly, the goal of reuniting the nation under the old duality, slave and free, became impossible, and a new goal, of abolishing slavery, became the explicit aim of the conflict. The Emancipation Proclamation in 1863 and the Thirteenth Amendment in 1865 would not have become part of American history without the actions of the slaves.

For the four million slaves freed at the end of the war, the period from 1865 to 1877 or so was a time of jubilation and hope, of an explosive release of creative energies, and then, almost before it had begun, of bitter disappointment and despair.

The exaltation with which the slaves greeted liberation put the lie to all the fairy tales of happy retainers strumming banjoes contentedly on the old plantation. For some of them, the response to the news of their freedom was immediate and visceral. The memories of that moment have gone into the folklore of African Americans. Here is one story of many that Leon Litwack tells in his luminous work, *Been in the Storm So Long*. It is the story of a slave named Caddy.

> Caddy had been sold to a man in Goodman, Mississippi. It was terrible to be sold in Mississippi. In fact, it was terrible to be sold anywhere. She had been put to work in the fields for running away again. She was hoeing a crop when she heard that General Lee had surrendered. Do you know who General Lee was? [This is her great-granddaughter speaking.] He was the man who was working for the South in the Civil War. When General Lee surrendered that meant that all the colored people were free! Caddy threw down that hoe, she marched herself up to the big house, then, she looked around and found her mistress. She went over to the mistress, she flipped up her dress and told the white woman to do something. She said it mean and ugly. This is what she said: *Kiss my ass!*

Despite their lack of formal education, the enslaved Negroes understood quite well the economics of their bondage. Some seem even to have had an intuitive grasp of John Locke's Labor Theory of Property. One man, learning that he was now free, walked into the big house on the plantation where he had labored as a slave for many years, and staked out a claim to the kitchen. I built it with my own hands, he said, and I figure that it is mine.

The Whites who had owned slaves desperately wanted them to go on working on the plantations even though they were no longer compelled to do so by law and by force. Cast in the unfamiliar role of supplicant, they vacillated between sweet offers of wages and kind treatment and dire warnings of the terrible fate that awaited their former slaves in the cold world of freedom. For the most part, we have only bits and snatches of reports of how all this appeared to the freedmen and women, but a few documents have come down to us that are extraordinarily revealing. The following very long letter, dictated by a former slave, is the most remarkable text I have come across in my continuing efforts to learn the story of the African-American experience. It is quite well known, and has appeared in several places. I think the author, Jourdon Anderson, is one of the great ironists of the American literary tradition.

Dayton, Ohio, August 7, 1865

To My Old Master, Colonel P. H. Anderson
Big Spring, Tennessee

Sir: I got your letter and was glad to find that you had not forgotten Jourdan, and that you wanted me to come back and live with you again, promising to do better for me than anybody else can. I have often felt uneasy about you. I thought the Yankees would have hung you long before this for harboring Rebs they found in your house. I suppose they never heard about your going to Col. Martin's to kill the Union soldier that was left by his company in their stable. Although you shot at me twice before I left you, I did not want to hear of your being hurt, and am glad you are still living. It would do me good to go back to the dear old home again and see Miss Mary and Miss Martha and Allen, Esther, Green, and Lee. Give my love to them all, and tell them I hope we will meet in the better world, if not in this. I would have gone back to see you all when I was working in the Nashville hospital, but one of the neighbors told me Henry intended to shoot me if he ever got a chance.

I want to know particularly what the good chance is you propose to give me. I am doing tolerably well here; I get $25 a month, with victuals and clothing; have a comfortable home for Mandy (the folks here call her Mrs. Anderson), and the children, Milly, Jane and Grundy, go to school and are learning well; the teacher says Grundy has a head for a preacher. They go to Sunday-School, and Mandy and me attend church regularly. We are kindly treated; sometimes we overhear others saying, "Them colored people were slaves" down in Tennessee. The children feel hurt when they hear such remarks, but I tell them it was no disgrace in Tennessee to belong to Col. Anderson. Many darkies would have been proud, as I used to was, to call you master. Now, if you will write and say what wages you will give me, I will be better able to decide whether it would be to my advantage to move back again. As to my freedom, which you say I can have, there is nothing to be gained on that score, as I got my free-papers in 1864 from the Provost-Marshal-General of the Department at Nashville. Mandy says she would be afraid to go back without some proof that you are sincerely disposed to treat us justly and kindly—and we have concluded to test your sincerity by asking you to send us our wages for the time we served you. This will make us forget and forgive old scores, and rely on your justice and friendship in the future. I served you faithfully for thirty-two years and Mandy twenty-years. At $25 a month for me, and $2 a week for Mandy, our earnings would amount to $11,680. Add to this the interest for the time our wages has been kept back and deduct what you paid for our clothing and three doctor's visits to me, and pulling a tooth for Mandy, and the balance will show what we are in justice entitled to. Please send the money by Adams Express, in care of V. Winters, esq. Dayton, Ohio. If you fail to pay us for faithful labors in the past we can have little faith in your promises in the future. We trust the good Maker has opened your eyes to the wrongs which you and your fathers have done to me and my fathers, in making us toil for you for generations without recompense. Here I draw my wages every Saturday night, but in Tennessee there was never any pay day for the negroes any more than for the horses and cows. Surely there will be a day of reckoning for those who defraud the laborer of his hire.

In answering the letter please state if there would be any safety for my Milly and Jane, who are now grown up and both good-looking girls. You know how it was with poor Matilda and Catherine. I would rather stay here and starve and die if it comes to that than have my girls brought to shame by the violence and wickedness of their young masters. You will also please state if there has been any schools opened for the colored children in your neighborhood, the great desire of my life now is to give my children an education, and have them form virtuous habits.

P.S.—Say howdy to George Carter, and thank him for taking the pistol from you when you were shooting at me.

> From your old servant,
> Jourdan Anderson

What was Jubilee for the liberated slaves was purgatory for their former masters. In the first chapter of *Capital*, Marx observes in a mock-philosophical footnote that "one man is a king only because other men stand in the relation of subjects to him. They, on the contrary, imagine that they are subjects because he is king." Much the same problem faced the wealthy White Southerners. Their conception of themselves as masters was possible only because there were others whom they could call slaves. When four million men and women ceased, by the signing of a surrender, to be slaves, the former masters no longer knew quite who or what they were.

To some extent, their discomfort was emotional. Accustomed from birth to deference, obedience, and at least the simulacrum of respect, they felt stripped naked by the loss of their slaves. But a more pressing problem was simply getting through the day. The pride of Southern chivalry suddenly found itself without cooks, cleaning ladies, seamstresses, carpenters, tailors, weavers, planters, reapers, threshers, bakers, and blacksmiths. Many of them allowed that they simply didn't know what to do. "I never did a day's work in my life," one gentleman acknowledged, "and don't know how to begin." "I am tired—tired tonight, will all the days of the year be like this one?" asked a flower of Southern womanhood. "What are we going to do without the negroes?"

The image of a genteel White Southern woman confronted with a cold stove and uncooked food or an unmade bed and dirty linens may bring a smile to our faces. *Schadenfreude*, the Germans call it. But it was not merely domestic comfort that was threatened by the freeing of the slaves. The entire economy of the South rested upon slave labor, and without the whip, the shackle, and legal title to their work force, White planters were uncertain how to obtain the labor they needed to till their fields. Once again, upper class Whites in America had to figure out how they were going to compel men and women to make a profit for them.

Both in America and elsewhere, entrepreneurs and their political supporters understood the situation quite well. Speaking not of the United States but of the British Caribbean empire, Viscount Howick stated openly the real problem posed by the emancipation of slaves.

> The great problem to be solved in drawing up a plan for the emancipation of the slaves in our colonies [he wrote in an 1832 memorandum] is to devise some mode of inducing them when relieved from the fear of the driver and his whip, to undergo the regular and continuous labour which is indispensable in carrying on the production of sugar.

In the United States following Emancipation, Southern Whites talked a good deal about the moral inadequacies of the Negro, who was loathe to "work" without the compulsion of slavery, but they all understood quite well what was really at stake. The freedmen and women were desperately eager to have the opportunity to work—*for themselves.* They wanted nothing more than land and farm implements with which they could grow their own food, supplement their harvest as their working-class White counterparts did with a little hunting and fishing, and perhaps even raise a cash crop to put some money in their pockets. The never-fulfilled promise of forty acres and a mule encapsulated their dream.

The freedmen were ready to work from sunup to sundown in their own fields, with their women beside them, if necessary, although they did *not* want their children to spend their days in the fields. Instead, they made it clear again and again that their fondest dream was for their children to get some education.

But a yeomanry supporting itself on its own land, however much that might be Jefferson's fantasied Ideal of the Land of Freedom, made no money for investors. The wealth of the Southern gentry rested on exploitable labor, of which they had just been deprived by Emancipation. Not surprisingly, the former slave masters immediately focused all their considerable talents, wealth, and political power on the task of reintroducing some form of bound labor into Southern society.

The problem of finding ways to exploit labor is not peculiar to slave societies, and while this drama was playing out in the South, a different form of exploitation—wage labor—was taking hold in the North. But the particularities of cash-crop agriculture posed special problems that led the plantation owners to take extraordinary measures. The first problem was that profitable large-scale cotton production, for example, required a kind of forced labor that was extremely harsh even by the standards of agricultural labor of the day. The freedmen and women knew what it was like to be marched in lockstep across a large field, with a driver whipping them to hoe, chop, and pick at an inhuman pace, and they wanted none of it. Some planters even offered extra wages for workers who were willing to do such work, and got few takers.

The second problem was that agriculture, unlike factory production, has a very long period of capital turnover. It may take a cloth manufacturer's workers no more than a few weeks to spin his wool or flax into thread and weave it, after which he can sell it and recoup his investment. But in agriculture, there is no payoff to the investor until the crop is harvested, many months later. It did a planter no good to hire a crew to plant and weed and hoe, only to have them leave for better jobs when harvest time came around. The dozen or so years after the end of the Civil War saw a succession of efforts by the planters to reestablish control over their labor force. Not surprisingly, the planters' first solution was naked force, backed by law—the solution that had stood them in such good stead during the long years of slavery. In collaboration with local legislators and law officers [who in many cases were the same], they imposed on the newly freed workers a system of Black Codes designed to force them to remain on the job, regardless of the conditions, until the crop was in and the profits were taken. Those Negroes found walking along the road could be charged with vagrancy, put in jail, and then rented out for a pittance to planters as convict labor. The shortage of reliable labor created a seller's market in some locations, with planters bidding against others of their class in attempts to fill out their work force. But night riders, lynching, burning, and mutilation brought the workforce around when economic incentives or legal constraints failed.

The freedmen were compelled to enter into labor contracts binding them to a particular plantation through the harvest season. Many of the labor contracts called for the Negroes' pay to be withheld until the crop was in. This tied them to the plantation in two ways: They forfeited an entire year's wages if they left before harvest, and in order to live, they were required to go into debt at a company store for food and necessaries. High prices, usurious rates of interest, and sheer cheating combined to bind many former slaves as securely as ever slavery had done.

The freedmen and women grasped perfectly what was being done to them and struggled with considerable effort and imagination to resist reenslavement. They tried, for example, to have the authorities declare their wages first in line in the claims against the proceeds from the crop, even before the claims of banks and local merchants. That way, if the crop fell short of expectations, as it did for three straight years after the end of the war, they would not be frozen out like the holders of second mortgages at a property auction.

For a while, they were helped by the Federal Government, which established a Bureau of Refugees, Freedmen, and Abandoned Lands one month before the surrender at Appomattox. The Freedmen's Bureau was administered by the conquering Northern army, and in some locales, it went to extraordinary lengths to guarantee basic economic rights for the former slaves. But with the failure of Congressional Reconstruction at the national level, the solidly entrenched power of the planters reasserted itself. Little by little, the efforts of the freedpeople to carve out lives for themselves as independent yeoman farmers were defeated by fraud, by theft, by violence, and by a network of oppressive and manipulative laws. Large numbers of the former slaves were forced into systems of sharecropping and debt peonage that differed only a little from the chattel slavery that the war had officially ended. Black workers who managed in a good year to get a bit ahead of their creditors and began to dream of their own farms were cheated of their earnings by crooked store owners, burned out by gangs of Whites, or simply murdered. In place of legal bondage, there was substituted, in the North as well as in the South, a caste system that sharply divided Whites from Blacks.

This system, to which the label Jim Crow is sometimes applied, persisted for at least one hundred years beyond the "liberation" ostensibly won by the North's victory in the Civil War. Now, in the first years of the fifth century of the presence of Africans in North America, America remains a house divided against itself.

A House Divided

The Revolutionary War and the Civil War are the two great markers dividing the American story into discrete chapters. Each chapter is a story in itself, with a beginning, a central theme, and a dramatic conclusion.

The first chapter is the Colonial period, which begins with the European colonization of North America and the building of a colonial empire on the foundation of unfree labor. Its central theme is the slow crystallization of the twin ideals of chattel slavery and free labor out of the original inchoate mixture of unfree labor. Its dramatic conclusion is the Revolutionary War. The second chapter is the antebellum period, which begins with the ratification of the Federal Constitution, sanctifying in the foundational document of the new nation the duality of Slavery and Freedom. Its central theme is the creation of a national society based on that duality, in which the two statuses, contradictory but inseparable from one another, define America during the first part of the nineteenth century. Its dramatic conclusion is the Civil War, which at first seemed to hold out the promise of overcoming the opposition of Slavery and Freedom by abolishing the first and extending the protections of the second to all Americans. Had that promise been kept, America would for the first time have become truly a Land of Freedom.

But the great promise of Emancipation was broken almost before the celebrations of Jubilee had died down. The four million slaves, freed by force of arms from their legal servitude, were driven by violence, by law, and by economic coercion back into the status of second-class citizens. They were stripped of the political rights they had scarcely begun to exercise, and their condition as exploitable labor was riveted to them as securely as ever their chains had been.

Now we must tell the third and most complex chapter of the new American story, a chapter that begins with the failure of Reconstruction. What is its theme, and will it have a dramatic conclusion?

When the four million slaves took off their shackles and walked out of bondage, they were, as a class, well prepared for the world of free labor in which henceforth they hoped to make their lives. Most of them had the agricultural skills that were greatly in demand, and many of them had craft skills suitable for small-scale production. Some even had experience as factory workers. For two hundred fifty years, they and their forebears had worked hard and well despite their unfreedom, building the Southern economy. The evidence of their skill was the wealth of the South, some regions of which had average per capita [White] incomes far above the national level. The products of their skill and energy stood all around them—mills, barns, forges, smokehouses, stately mansions and the furniture that filled them. No enslaved people has ever left slavery better prepared to take its place in the world of free labor.

This is not the traditional story, of course. For almost a century and a half now, both the friends and the enemies of the Negro have described the liberated slaves as an illiterate, unskilled *lumpenproletariat* completely unprepared for their freedom. Those who today are sympathetic to the economic plight of African Americans argue that the disabilities visited on their ancestors by slavery have so disadvantaged them that some sort of affirmative assistance is required if they are to be lifted to the level of White workers. Those who are unsympathetic argue that one hundred thirty-five years should have been enough time for the Negro to pull himself together and develop the moral character, skills, and work habits exhibited by his more successful White counterpart. We have here what was labeled an Antinomy by Immanuel Kant more than two centuries ago in his *Critique of Pure Reason*—that is, an argument in which both sides reach false conclusions because they begin with a common false premise. The freedmen and women were *not* unprepared for the new world of free labor. Indeed, the common opinion during the last days of slavery was that the slaves were *good* workers—hard-working, efficient, capable of learning new techniques quickly. That is why they brought such a high price at auction and were in demand on plantations and in factories. Southern White workers had a generally bad reputation among employers, who considered them [whether justifiably or not] lazy, careless, and unproductive. A generation later, the common opinion had completely reversed itself. All the negative characteristics that had been attached to poor Whites in the ante-bellum South were now imputed to Negroes, while the stock of the Southern White worker rose.

What actually occurred during the two or three generations following Emancipation was a progressive *de-skilling* of the Black work force. Black workers were denied access to any but the most menial jobs in the free labor market, for now they were competing against White workers. As Jacqueline Jones says in *American Work*, to which so much of my own understanding of these matters is indebted,

> Whites in general believed not that black people were incapable of doing jobs which so many other poor workers obviously managed to master, but rather that they should not be allowed to do those jobs.

In the last decades of the nineteenth century, and again during World War I, tens of thousands of Black workers left the Southern farms and plantations and moved northward to try their luck in the big cities. Chicago, New York, Detroit, Philadelphia—all saw their Black populations soar as this steady migration continued. There were jobs in the industrializing North, but the situation for Black workers was fully as bad as it was in the South. Black workers were entirely excluded from certain industries. When they *were* hired, it was always in the lowest paid, least skilled, most onerous and dangerous jobs, and regardless of what skills they acquired, they were denied advancement. White labor unions, which were beginning to form at this time, shut them out, while admitting waves of European immigrants who were, after all, just as much competitors for scarce jobs. Employers, who might have been ready to lower wage levels by offering advancement to desperate Black workers, bowed to the demands of their own White workers and traded slightly higher wages for labor peace. Rather than risk strikes by White workers determined to keep Black workers out, they established what was in effect a racially encoded two-tier job structure.

Some jobs, of course, were reserved for Black workers. The porters on the Pullman sleeping cars were Black men, required to reenact the antebellum fantasies of the Southern plantation for those traveling by train. Many of the porters were educated men with college degrees, blocked by the racial coding of the work world from ever finding jobs commensurate with their accomplishments. In the White world, sleeping car porters were merely servants in uniform, but they were often leaders in the Black communities, pillars of their churches or fraternal organizations.

On one occasion, W. E. B. Du Bois was traveling by train—consigned to a car reserved for Coloreds. [John Bracey tells this story, to show how well known Du Bois was in the Black world.] He was not permitted to eat in the dining car, of course, but a sleeping car porter brought him a meal carefully laid out on a tray, with napery and silver. "No one will ever say that Dr. Du Bois was denied a meal on *this* train," he said.

The situation of Black women was even worse, needless to say. On the plantations, they had worked in the fields alongside the men—the chivalry of the slave owners did not extend to their property. After Emancipation, Black women entered the labor market earlier and in larger numbers than their White counterparts. But like Black men, they were denied access even to jobs that White workers might consider quite inferior. Before liberation, Whites were more than happy to be waited on in public by Black slaves. After liberation, they could not stomach the idea of being served in a department store or a restaurant by a Black salesperson or waitress. Black women, some with college degrees, were closed out of such jobs until well after the Second World War. Instead, they were forced to line up at street corners early in the morning so that White women looking for domestic servants could offer them day work at miserable wages. For generations of Black families, dinner often consisted of leavings and scraps from White dinner tables, brought home by those women on "the plate."

Black workers struggled to gain entry to the industries that offered steady work and good wages. When they succeeded in fighting their way in, it was usually only as the industry was on the way down, losing jobs either to technological change or to overseas outsourcing. Never were Black workers admitted to the industries on the cutting edge, those that were growing, expanding, offering security and good salaries for the future.

During the two and a half centuries *before* the Civil War, Americans were segregated into two distinct racially coded castes—one increasingly free and secure in its rights, the other progressively more enslaved and deprived of all rights. This division was mandated by legislation, by judicial decision, and eventually by the Federal Constitution itself. It was what lawyers call *de jure*. After the Civil War, which ended the *de jure* division of America into two castes, a new division of Americans was introduced into the world of work, drawn exactly along the same racial lines. White workers had access to jobs, to advancement, to the capital needed to start businesses; Black workers were denied that access. Thus what had been done in law before, was now accomplished in fact—*de facto*. America was still a Land of Freedom and Bondage.

On June 17, 1858, Abraham Lincoln gave a speech in Springfield, Illinois, as part of his campaign against Stephen Douglas for the Senate. Speaking of the slavery controversy, he uttered these famous words: "A house divided against itself cannot stand." Lincoln was wrong. America had stood divided against itself for two hundred fifty years, and it would continue to stand, divided against itself, for one hundred fifty more.

As White legislators, judges, employers, and workers imposed an inferior status on Black men and women in the world of work, White Americans did everything in their power to consign Black Americans as a whole to a second-class status in society. There had been no need for Whites constantly to reinforce the inferior status of Black people under slavery. The fact of legal bondage created an unbridgeable gulf between Whites and Blacks that permitted Whites to adopt a relatively more relaxed attitude toward the slaves. If you were White, you could chat with, play with, even make love with Blacks, secure in the knowledge that you could the next moment strike them, whip them, or sell them down the river. But once Black people were legally free, it became a matter of obsessive, even hysterical importance for Whites repeatedly and publicly to confirm their superior status.

The most effective mechanism for this ritual assertion of superiority was brutal force. So long as Black workers were slaves, the White masters had an economic interest in seeing to it that the violence visited upon them did not go so far as to end their lives or so badly cripple them that they could no longer work. Slaves were an extremely expensive investment, and by the 1860s, their value had increased considerably. Collectively, the slave population constituted fully one half of the entire wealth of the White South. That wealth was routinely used to secure agricultural loans, pay debts, settle estates, and serve as a reservoir of assets against the danger of a bad harvest or an unwise business decision. A healthy mature Black male slave could bring as much as fifteen hundred dollars at auction—perhaps four or five times the annual wage of a Northern free laborer. It is hardly surprising that three quarters of Southern Whites owned no slaves at all.

With the end of slavery, Whites no longer had anything to lose economically from inflicting torture, mutilation, maiming, and death on Black people, and with the system of local justice firmly in their control, they faced little or nothing in the way of legal penalties either. So it was that they unleashed on the freedmen and women what we might wish to call a Reign of Terror—except that that period in the French Revolution did not come close to the horrors of lynching. For the space of fifty years, a Black man, woman, or child was lynched on an average of once every two and a half days.

These are difficult matters to speak about even now. The traditional image of a lynching is of a Black man hanged by the neck from a tree, and there were, to be sure, many such deaths. But that image does not even begin to capture the sheer sadistic inhumanity routinely exhibited by decent White townspeople at the public lynchings. Advertisements were taken out in local newspapers announcing forthcoming lynchings. Black victims were burned alive. Their fingers, toes, and genitalia were cut off by excited on-lookers and taken home as souvenirs. Picture postcards were made up from photographs of the dead bodies. Nothing in the horrific accounts of the Nazi holocaust surpasses the obscenity of this quintessentially American form of public amusement. I find it difficult to maintain an appropriate authorial self-control when writing of these events, but a decent respect for the victims requires that I incorporate at least one description of a lynching into this narrative. Those who wish to pursue the matter further are urged to read the chapter entitled "Hellhounds" in Leon Litwack's great work, *Trouble in Mind*, and then to reflect on what the constant reality of the threat of such treatment must do to the mind of any Black man or woman in America.

> The brutalities meted out in these years often exceeded the most vivid of imaginations. After learning of the lynching of her husband, Mary Turner—in her eighth month of pregnancy—vowed to find those responsible, swear out warrants against them, and have them punished in the courts. For making such a threat, a mob of several hundred men and women determined to "teach her a lesson." After tying her ankles together, they hung her from a tree, head downward. Dousing her clothes with gasoline, they burned them from her body. While she was still alive, someone used a knife ordinarily reserved for splitting hogs to cut open the woman's abdomen. The infant fell prematurely from her womb to the ground and cried briefly, whereupon a member of the Valdosta, Georgia mob crushed the baby's head beneath his heel. Hundreds of bullets were then fired into Mary Turner's body, completing the work of the mob. The Associated Press, in its notice of the affair, observed that Mary Turner had made "unwise remarks" about the execution of her husband, "and the people, in their indignant mood, took exception to her remarks, as well as her attitude."

A student in a seminar asked John Bracey one day why W. E. B. Du Bois had been able to develop into so strong and original a scholar despite the impediments placed in the way of Black people in the years just after the Civil War. John suggested the answer might lie in the fact that Du Bois grew up in Great Barrington, Massachusetts, and hence was not haunted every day of his youth by the knowledge that if he spoke too freely or at the wrong moment, he might be set upon by a White mob and tortured to death. We will never know, he observed, how many other great minds were prematurely stilled in the South. Along with the brutalities of lynching went the daily constraints and indignities of Jim Crow—separate and unequal toilets, separate and unequal access to theaters and restaurants, separate and unequal seating in public transportation. In every way that they could devise, Whites set Blacks aside and forced them into a separate and inferior world.

Much is made in these days of feel-good popular psychology of the injuries done to the Negro ego by this constant barrage of bad vibrations, but that trivializes and misrepresents what was being done. To be sure, none of us is immune to self-doubts when the world tells us every day that we are worthless. But Black people had survived two hundred fifty years of slavery without losing their belief in their own worthiness, as their rebellions, their resistances, their music, their religion, and their folklore demonstrate. What is noteworthy is not that on occasion they got to singing the blues, but that despite everything White people could think to do to them, they persevered.

The main problem with second-class jobs, after all, isn't that they constitute an assault on one's self-esteem. It is that they are more dangerous and harder, and they pay less and offer less in the way of job security. The problem with segregated toilets, if you are Black, is that they are few and far between. It was a White fantasy that Black people lusted after intimate association with them. Mostly, Black people just wanted a place to sit down when they were tired, a restaurant in which to eat when they were hungry, and a decent bathroom to use when they needed it.

So long as America had an agricultural economy, Whites needed as much Black labor as they could buy, breed, or steal. Agriculture was, until very recently, extremely labor intensive. In a nation with virtually endless arable land, there was always more money to be made if you could only lay your hands on more workers. On the plantations, during the slow parts of the growing cycle, masters had no trouble finding other things for the slaves to do. They could construct and repair farm buildings, work in the big house, cure ham, make molasses, grow their own food, and make their own clothing. All of these productive activities contributed to the general profitability of the plantation. After the Civil War, the former slave owners were desperate to get the freedmen and women to work for them. Without a reliable supply of labor, their land was useless to them.

The industrial expansion in the North also created a need for labor. Indeed, a free labor market works best, from the point of view of the employers, when there is a *surplus* of workers, whose job searches drive down wages and so increase profits. As I noted, Northern industrialists actively sought Black workers from the South, prompting a wave of migrations.

One of the paradoxes of the post–Civil War era is that it saw the development of a *greater* degree of distance between the races than had existed under slavery. The physical closeness of slaves and masters gave way to an increasing separation. In the North, Black people were segregated in urban communities from which they found it impossible to move even if they had the money to afford better housing.

At first, these all-Black sections of the big Northern cities were vibrant and functional working-class neighborhoods, with a wide range of small Black-owned establishments—beauty parlors, funeral parlors, shops, restaurants, pool halls, churches, newspapers, and even, on occasion, local banks. There were networks of social relationships that knitted the neighborhoods together, and although the inhabitants were economically consigned to the lowest level jobs, these neighborhoods functioned successfully as communities. But as the structure of the American economy shifted after World War II, the jobs at the low end of the economy began to disappear. At the same time, the growth of all-White suburbs radically changed the racial composition of the big Northern cities. Just as Blacks gained admission to industrial jobs only when those industries were declining, so Blacks gained access to urban political power only when Mayors were losing the tax base they needed to support programs for their constituents.

Why didn't the Blacks in the cities move to the suburbs and buy homes? Were they too carefree and spendthrift to save the money needed for a down payment? Did they lack family values, the desire to have a home of their own on which they could lavish care and attention? Did they suffer from a ghetto mentality?

Well, one reason is that White people deliberately adopted the policy of denying them the mortgages they needed to get a start. In 1934, in the depths of the Depression, the Federal Government established the Federal Housing Authority for the explicit purpose of underwriting home ownership. The FHA put out an *Underwriting Manual* as a guide to its loan officers in selecting suitable families for mortgage loans. As a matter of official government policy, the manual directed loan officers *not* to extend loans to Black applicants. Here is the language of the manual: "if a neighborhood is to maintain stability, it is necessary that properties shall continued to be occupied by the same social and racial classes." The manual recommended "restrictive covenants" as a useful device for preserving residential racial purity. One result of this policy, which was in force until February 15, 1950, was that all 82,000 residents of the famous Long Island suburban development, Levittown, were White. The impact of this discriminatory policy has reached across half a century beyond its official termination, depriving Black families unto the third generation of an equal stake in the rising American economy. Prompted by the analysis by Melvin Oliver and Thomas Shapiro of the enormous gap between the assets of Black households and those of White households, I worked out a little thought experiment to demonstrate just how far-reaching the continuing effects of past discrimination can be.

I am going to trace the asset accumulations of two lower-middle class American families over a thirty-year period. The first family is Joe and Mary Smith, who are White, and their two children, Skip and Jane.

The second family is William and Esther Robinson, who are Black, and their two children, Michael and Carolyn.

In 1950, after World War II, the Smiths buy a small house in a new suburban community, aided by an FHA insured mortgage. They pay $10,500, and secure a thirty year 6% fixed rate loan for $10,000, the remainder scraped together from money Joe has saved in the army. William Robinson has also saved $500 from his army pay, but he is denied a loan under the Federal Government's explicit and official policies of racial discrimination. Unable to buy a home, the Robinsons rent an apartment for their family, at an initial rental of $120 a month.

Both Joe Smith and Bill Robinson find jobs in post–World War II America, and they make, let us suppose, exactly the same wage. What is more, let us imagine that over the next thirty years they get identical raises, and are never out of work. Now let us trace over a thirty-year period the housing expenditures and asset formation of the Smith family and the Robinson family. I am going to make some reasonable simplifying assumptions about changes in rental rates, insurance rates, and real estate taxes, and also about the savings propensities of families with disposable income. Let us see what happens to the Smiths and the Robinsons. Remember—the families have identical starting assets, they are the same age, they have equivalent jobs, they get the same raises, and—I shall assume—have identically stable homes with identically responsible and committed bread-winners.

The Smiths first. The annual cost of a 6% fixed rate 30-year mortgage is $72/1000, or $720 a year. Since this is a fixed rate mortgage, that amount never changes over the entire thirty-year period of the loan, despite the fact that between 1950 and 1980, the Consumer Price Index rose by 341%. [The CPI for housing actually rose more than that, but let us keep this simple.]

In the thirty-year period from 1950 through 1979, Joe and Mary Smith pay out a total of $21,600 in monthly mortgage payments. They also pay insurance and real estate taxes, of course. I will assume that taxes and insurance start at $260 a year, and rise slowly to $1300 a year by the time the mortgage is paid off at the start of 1980. Suppose these items, over thirty years, total $22,550.

So, in thirty years the Smiths spend $44,150 on housing.

But much of that is tax deductible, thanks to federal policies designed to encourage home ownership. For example, $11,600 of the mortgage payments is interest [the total paid out less the original loan]. In addition, roughly $17,500 of the taxes plus insurance is deductible real estate taxes.

So over the years, the Smiths have enjoyed a $29,100 tax deduction, which we will assume, at an average marginal rate of 25%, returns to them $7,275. Thus, the net cost to the Smiths of housing has been $36,875.

The Smiths put $2,000 of this tax break in the bank, and spend the rest on such things as college educations for their children, Skip and Jane.

In 1980, the Smiths have a bank account of $2,400 [including bank interest], and a home which they own free and clear. In the intervening thirty years, real estate has soared, and their little house, even though thirty years old, is now worth $50,000 on the housing market. So the total assets of the Smiths add up to $52,400.

Meanwhile the Robinsons have been living in their apartment and paying rents that rise steadily, thanks to inflation. In 1950, they pay $120 a month for their apartment, but over thirty years, the rent rises to $350. [This is of course a *very* modest assumption. Real rents have risen considerably more.] Assuming a schedule of gradual rises, we can estimate that at the end of thirty years, the Robinsons have paid a total of $82,200 for housing. This is $43,325 more than the Smiths paid, even though the Smiths were paying off the mortgage on their home, and the Robinsons were renting an apartment.

What assets have the Robinsons accumulated in thirty years? The simple answer is *none*. They have had no tax breaks from their rental payments, they do not own the apartment in which they have lived for thirty years, and because of their rising rents, they have been unable to save a portion of Mr. Robinson's salary.

Thus, purely as a consequence of discriminatory policies adopted explicitly by the Federal Government in the 1930s, the Smiths, who are White, have net assets of $52,400 in 1980, and the Robinsons, who are Black, have net assets of zero.

The long-term effects of the original discrimination do not end here, however. They are transmitted to the next generation—to Skip and Jane and Michael and Carolyn [all of whom, note, have grown up in stable, secure lower-middle-class homes with two parents and good family values].

First of all, the Smiths have been able to divert a considerable portion of their income to the education of their children, because of the beneficial laws and policies governing housing. This advantage shows up in the higher incomes the Smith children are able to earn, as compared with the equally talented, but less-well-educated Robinson children.

Secondly, the Smiths are in a position to make available to their children the advantages of home ownership. By 1980, when Skip is thirty-two, housing has risen so much that a new small house costs $100,000, not

$10,000. Skip needs a $10,000 down payment to secure a mortgage loan, and even though he has a good job—better than his father was ever able to obtain—he simply cannot save the $10,000 out of his paycheck. But his father can now help him out. Refinancing the family home, which the Smiths now own outright, Joe Smith takes a $10,000 mortgage and gives his son [tax free] the down payment. In effect, the Smiths are advancing a portion of the children's inheritance to them in this form. Skip buys a home, and begins to enjoy all the advantages that his parents were able to secure thirty years earlier.

Michael, on the other hand, even though he has as good a job as Skip, will never be able to buy his own home, for his father has no assets that may be deployed to give him the down payment. The disadvantages of the fathers are visited upon the sons. Thoughtless social commentators will wonder why Skip is doing so much better by the year 2000 than Michael is, and will come up with elaborate cultural and psychological explanations, blaming low self-esteem [if they are liberals] or the lack of a suitable work ethic [if they are conservatives], but all of their fancy explanations will be wrong. The real explanation is the generations-long effects of explicitly discriminatory policies of previous eras, which continue to manifest themselves in dramatic inequalities of wealth, even after inequalities in income have been corrected by the marketplace or even by affirmative action and anti-discrimination laws.

This is one story—many others could be told—that shows the persistent effects of the four centuries old division of American society into two unequal racial groups. Some while ago, I came across a story in the *New York Times* about a study that shows that Black buyers of Nissan cars consistently pay considerably more than White customers for their car loans (*New York Times*, 4 July, 2001—Independence Day). There are countless such systematic disadvantages built into the fabric of American society, which taken all together more than account for the disaparities between the wealth accumulation of Black and White families.

Joe and Mary Smith are hard-working people who have a very keen sense of entitlement to the secure and comfortable life they have built for themselves and their children. In their eyes, people like Bill and Esther Robinson—if, indeed, the Smiths ever take notice of them—must be irresponsible, or wasteful, or lacking in Middle Class values, if after thirty years they still live in an apartment and cannot afford to send their children to college. The politicians who represent Joe and Mary Smith, from their City Councillor all the way up to the President of the United States, tell them as much every chance they get.

Bill and Esther Robinson see the American story differently. They recall quite vividly the day on which Bill was turned down for an FHA-secured home mortgage. The Smiths, if they were told about that event from the distant past, would probably wonder why the Robinsons insist on dwelling on ancient history. After all, the policy they blame for their lack of assets was reversed ages ago. The Robinsons know differently. Fifty years ago, when I was a young Sophomore at Harvard, Carl Sandburg came to lecture. New Lecture Hall was packed to the rafters, and I was barely able to find a spot to stand in the aisle. He sang a few songs and read a bit from *The People, Yes*, and then he told a story about two cockroaches.

It seems that these two cockroaches were brothers, and they were riding into the city on the back of a truck one day when the truck hit a bump. One brother fell on top of a dung heap, and the other fell down a sewer drain. Now, a dung heap is very heaven to a cockroach, and that brother waxed fat and prospered. He just sat on that dung heap for a year, getting bigger and shinier. The other brother nearly drowned, and spent the same year slowly, painfully dragging himself out of the sewer back onto the street. By the time he got there, he was emaciated and his shell was mottled and sickly looking. Looking around, he saw his brother on top of the dung heap, and greeted him. "Brother," he said, "look at you! I am half-dead, and down to a third of my normal weight. You are fat and shiny and fine looking. How on earth did you get so prosperous?" His brother looked down at him, preened himself, and replied, "Brains. And hard work."

As the post–World War II period unfolded, a surplus of Black workers developed in America because of changes in the economy. In the eyes of many Whites, that surplus constituted a threat to social peace and order. White America responded in three ways to this perceived threat. First, they created a system of social welfare payments designed to take the edge off inner-city poverty and joblessness in the hope that that would keep rebellions from breaking out. Second, they offered Black men and women jobs in the military, where they could earn a decent working-class wage, get food, housing, and medical care, and be under constant supervision, while risking their lives for White America. And third, they locked up a million Blacks at a time, mostly men, in a vast system of prisons. This last solution had the side benefit of making a large segment of the Black population ineligible to vote, thereby reintroducing some measure of Black disenfranchisement—one of the principal goals of Southern Whites at the close of Reconstruction.

Derrick Bell explored the idea that White America no longer needs Blacks in a lovely short story called "The Space Traders." Bell imagines that aliens arrive from space and offer America untold riches in return for all of its African Americans, whom they intend to take back to their home world. I don't think I will spoil the impact of the story for anyone who has not yet read it if I tell you that in the end, after much deliberation and debate, White America accepts the offer. The last sentence of the story is worth quoting: "Heads bowed, arms now linked by slender chains, black people left the new world as their forebears had arrived."

Bell is suggesting that America no longer needs or wants the people it brought here from Africa by force. But that is not quite true, as I think Bell would readily agree, for White America still does have a need for Black people—White America needs to be able to reassure itself and congratulate itself that it is not Black. After Emancipation, the White gentry in the South secured the political support of poor Whites, whose economic interests were sometimes completely opposed to those of the gentry, by calling on them to make a united front against Blacks. In the North, employers divided their labor force along racial lines as a way of stopping them from organizing strong unions. Only twenty years ago, Reagan won the support of poor Whites whose pockets were being plucked by his economic policies—once again, using race as a way of uniting Whites.

One of the odd signs of this racial subtext of modern American politics is the constant appeal by both major parties to "Middle Class Americans." A few facts and figures can put the subject in perspective. According to the Bureau of Labor Statistics, there are about one hundred million people in America who work full-time earning wages or salaries. (That doesn't include the self-employed.) About fifty-two million of them earn $30,000 a year or less. This fifty-two million includes sixty-six percent of all Black workers and seventy-four percent of all Hispanic workers. Now, anyone who actually pays the bills in a household these days knows that $30,000 doesn't buy a middle class life. Most workers earn only about half of what it takes to maintain anything resembling middle class life. For most American families, the only way to ascend to the middle class is to send at least two people from the household into the work world.

Here is a question. Every Black person in America knows the answer, but it seems as though it is almost impossible for White people to figure it out. With half of working Americans earning wages that at best pay for a working class existence, why do politicians focus all their attention on Middle Class Americans?

Here is the answer: In America today, Middle Class means *not Black*. When I was young, White people would say, "I can do what I please. I am free, White, and twenty-one!" Today, those same people or their children and grandchildren insist that they are Middle Class, meaning that they are not Black and do not live in a ghetto.

For four centuries, White people in America have defined their freedom by contrasting it with the unfreedom of others. At the very beginning, the line between freedom and bondage was color-blind, but very quickly, it took on a racial hue. Before the Civil War, to be Black was to be unfree by law; to be White was to be free. After Emancipation, the racial line between freedom and unfreedom has remained. Only the mechanisms for enforcing it have changed.

America was born as a Land of Freedom and Bondage, and it remains to this day a Land of Freedom and Bondage.

And so my story is done. This is the story my colleagues taught me in the W. E. B. Du Bois Department of Afro-American Studies. It is the story I learned from reading that pile of fifty books, and all the other books my colleagues have gently suggested I might take a look at. It is the story I have come to understand not just by reading and listening, but by accepting the invitation to join a Black Studies Department and joining my fortunes with those of men and women who have spent their lives in the struggle for racial justice.

It is not the inspiring fairy tale of America the Land of Freedom, nor is it the self-congratulatory story of American Exceptionalism, but it is a true story, and a better narrative suit of clothes for Uncle Sam.

It has a theme, but it has no dramatic conclusion, for America remains a land of bondage and liberty, in which those who are free define their freedom by its contrast to the bondage of those who are unfree. I have no proposals for reform, or for revolt. I am telling a story, not drafting a blueprint. But I am sure of this: Until White America puts away the old story that it has told itself for centuries, and learns this new story of its past and its present, it will be unable to understand itself and will have no hope of finally bringing this sad story to an end.

4

THE AMERICAN GRIOT

Who will tell this story? Who will be responsible for keeping it alive in our national conversation from generation to generation? In the traditional societies of West Africa, the task would have fallen to the *Griot*. The Griot was a singer, a teller of tales, an historian, a genealogist, the bearer of the collective memory of the people. He or she—though it was most often a man—would learn by heart the epic stories of the origins of the people, of their great rulers and famous battles. Trained as an acolyte and apprentice by the older Griots, he would sing the old stories at feasts and celebrations, embellishing them with barbed and witty comments about recent events. Among some African peoples, the Griot was revered and feared, among others despised and outcast, but without him, the people would soon have forgotten their past, and so would have ceased to be a people.

America is a literate society, with books and archives and videotapes of inaugurations and funerals. It would seem that we have no need for the Griot. And yet, we do need singers of our national story who will commit their lives to remembering what we have been and what we have done.

Who will tell the real story of America? For many years, the task fell to a scattering of scholars who labored in the vineyards of historiography, all but ignored by White America—William Edward Burghardt Du Bois, perhaps the greatest social scientist, White or Black, ever to appear on the American scene; Carter Woodson, who founded the Association for the Study of Negro Life and History; Arthur Schomburg, whose vast collection of documents, papers, and artifacts now makes the Schomburg Library in New York an essential resource for the study of the Black experience. The story was told by novelists as well, by Richard Wright, whose collection of short stories, *Uncle Tom's Children*, matches but cannot surpass the horror of the newspaper accounts of lynchings; and by Zora Neale Hurston and James Baldwin and many, many more.

Having had the privilege for more than a decade of membership in a Department of Afro-American Studies, I have come to believe that the sacred responsibility of the Griot in America has fallen to Black Studies as a discipline and to the scholars who now serve as Professors of that discipline. Many other scholars and artists play the role of Griot, but in a society like ours, which institutionalizes every social role and assigns to it titles, degrees, and the other stigmata of public acceptability, the discipline of Black Studies has an indispensable part to play in the telling of the true American story.

What is Black Studies?

It is time to take a closer look at Black Studies. Before we can decide whether it is suited to play the role of the American Griot, we need to understand a bit more about how it came into existence in the modern university, and where it is now headed. I have talked at length with my colleagues, who were there at the creation and played a role in determining what Black Studies has become. They have helped me to understand that not everything that has gone by the name Black Studies in the past thirty-odd years fits the role of the American Griot.

In 1968, America's college and university campuses erupted into protest, as Black students, newly admitted to formerly lily-white schools, demanded that *their* history, *their* art, *their* literature, the breadth and depth of *their* experiences and those of their ancestors be admitted into the curriculum. Terrified by the rebellions in the cities, and by campus protests triggered by the murder of Martin Luther King, anxious to maintain campus order and at least the simulacrum of racial sensitivity, presidents, provosts, deans, and faculties hustled about conjuring up a response to the demands. To anyone familiar with the glacial pace of change in the academy, the response seemed blindingly fast. Within three years, close to five hundred Institutes, Programs, Committees, Degrees, and Departments of Black Studies, Africana Studies, or Afro-American Studies had been established.

Pride of place as the first Black Studies program in America is traditionally awarded to San Francisco State, where several years of protest and negotiation led in 1968 to the establishment of a full-scale Black Studies curriculum consisting of eleven courses in the Humanities and Social

Sciences, in a department headed by Nathan Hare. But five years earlier, at Merritt College (in Oakland, California), Huey Newton, Bobby Seale, and other members of Merritt's Afro-American Society forced the college briefly to adopt a Black history course.

The response to the protests was for the most part disingenuous, temporizing, and calculated to be as easily reversed as it had been initiated. Once the cities stopped burning and the students stopped marching, the tide of Black Studies receded. Quite rapidly, the number of programs shrank to perhaps two hundred. Nevertheless, those two hundred persisted, and a third of a century later, they are firmly established as a part of the Arts and Sciences curriculum. More recently, scholars have begun to create doctoral programs—always the true sign of success for a discipline in the academy. First at Temple University, then at the University of Massachusetts Amherst, later at Berkeley and Yale, just recently at Harvard, a serious student can pursue a doctorate and enter on a career of scholarship and teaching in Black Studies or Afro-American Studies.

No sooner had Afro-American Studies sprung into being than it came under attack, both from inside and outside the academy. A few of the attacks were simply uninformed—like Saul Bellow's famous sneer that when someone showed him a Zulu *War and Peace* he would be prepared to admit the legitimacy of studying African Literature. Often the objection to Afro-American Studies was that its entry into the academic community had been political in its motivation, and hence that it was unsuited to take its place among the pure, disinterested disciplines whose only ambition was the pursuit of knowledge.

More recently, a somewhat hysterical attack has been launched against what is commonly called "multi-culturalism," by Stephen and Abigail Thernstrom, Arthur Schlesinger, Jr., Lynne Cheney, and Dinesh D'Souza. They are still in the grip of the fantasy that America exhibits a magical unity that makes it a model and inspiration to the world, and they warn anxiously of the corruption of learning and the end of the university if we stop telling the old story.

In the ferment of the early years of the discipline, scores of manifestos, defenses, explanations, and proposals were published, with a wide variety of goals. The early founders and proponents of Black Studies were almost unanimous in insisting on a *political* dimension to the new discipline. They called on Black Studies to provide support and comfort to Black students enrolled at formerly all-white institutions. They demanded that the new programs establish and maintain close connections to northern urban Black communities, near which many of the colleges and universities were located. Some of the most prominent leaders even wanted Black Studies on the campuses to offer practical training for social action. Higher education, they hoped, would serve as a staging ground for revolution.

There was one demand that came most immediately and forcefully from the Black students themselves. Being admitted at long last in significant numbers to previously all-White campuses, they looked at the course offerings and reading assignments and asked, Where are we in all of this? Where are the men and women who labored under slavery, and struggled against it? Where are the poets, the novelists, the playwrights, the composers, the painters, the sculptors, the scientists, the entertainers whose genius has enriched American culture? Are there no Black historians, philosophers, sociologists, political theorists, politicians, or religious leaders in the entire sweep of American history? Where are the Black labor leaders, the visionaries, the revolutionaries?

At the very least, they pleaded, add a Black novelist or two to a course on American Literature. If nothing else, spend a few weeks on the story of slavery in a year-long introduction to American History. When telling the story of the Civil War and Reconstruction, allow the voice of W. E. B. Du Bois to balance the voices of the apologists for slavery.

Here, for example, is a Black historian, Roger Fischer, writing in 1969.

American literature courses meandered from Michael Wigglesworth to J. D. Salinger without acknowledging the poems of Lawrence Dunbar or the novels of James Baldwin. Music professors blandly attributed the origins of jazz to Paul Whiteman. Few dramatics courses interrupted their readings of hallowed classics to pay any attention to Lorraine Hansbury's brilliant *Raisin in the Sun*. All too often, the only Negroes encountered in studies of American culture were little Topsy, Uncle Remus, and those docile darkies of *Green Pastures*, Sambo stereotypes created by white writers for white readers. United States history courses ignored the African heritage so completely it seemed to Lerone Bennett as if 'black Americans appear suddenly by a process of spontaneous generation.' Negroes merited attention in American history surveys only when they were making trouble or when white agitators were doing so on their behalf. Ten Jeffersonians arrested under the Alien and Sedition decrees often received as much time as and more sympathy than four million enslaved blacks. Instructors spent weeks discussing the white immigrant ghettos of the nineteenth century, then ignored Harlem, Hough, and Watts altogether.

From the enlightened perspective of the Third Millennium, we might imagine that it would be impossible even to consider turning down a simple request for the inclusion of the African-American experience in university curricula. The academy, after all, conceives itself as embodying the exalted vision of classical Greece and Rome. Was it not the Roman playwright Terence who said "Homo sum. Humani nil a me alienum" (I am a man. Nothing human is alien to me.) But alas, even so modest and respectful a request had to submit to full-scale scholarly review by the guardians of Western Civilization, and the outcome was by no means certain.

In 1967, the Black Student Alliance at Yale, led by Armstead Robinson, began to argue for some sort of incorporation of Black Studies into the undergraduate curriculum. As Robinson tells it, "after several months of determined effort, we discovered that little progress was being made in the struggle to convince the faculty at large of the validity and importance of our concerns." At the symposium organized by the students, the Provost began by making a few suitably sensitive remarks about racism and the like, and then with quite unconscious condescension, posed the question to which the speakers would address themselves: "What is the intellectual significance of focusing a part of our curriculum consciously and directly on the black experience?" Or, as President Brewster put it in one early discussion, "Is race a proper organizing principle for the curriculum?"

That same year, our old friend Thomas A. Bailey delivered his presidential address to the annual meeting of the Organization of American Historians. Speaking on "the mythmakers of American history," Bailey took some potshots at a variety of "myths," ranging from the cherry tree story about George Washington to George Bancroft's celebration of Andrew Jackson. He then turned his critical gaze on a "newly formed hyphenate group," African-Americans, and offered the following opinion:

This belated recognition [of the experiences and activities of Negroes], though praiseworthy in some respects, is fraught with danger. Most non-militant Negroes would probably like to think of themselves as dark-skinned Americans, and this self-imposed Jim Crowism can be self-defeating. Pressure-group history of any kind is deplorable, *especially when significant white men are bumped out to make room for much less significant black men in the interests of social harmony.* [emphasis added] If this kind of distortion gets completely out of hand, we can visualize what will happen when the Negroes become the dominant group in all our largest cities, as they already are in Washington, D.C. Coexistence may end, and we may even have hard-backed Negro histories of the United States, with the white man's achievements relegated to a subsidiary treatment.

Apparently the White male backlash does not limit itself to the supposed sufferings of *living* White men. Even dead White men—*significant* dead White men no less—may fail to receive their due if the militancy of African Americans is not kept in check.

But more than thirty years have passed, and it looks as though this is one battle we may actually have won. Black authors *are* regularly included on the required reading lists of college and university courses. Not merely the doings of prominent Black men and women, but the lives and activities of the millions of less prominent African Americans crop up in history courses outside of Afro-American Studies departments.

While writing these lines, I paused to access the on-line descriptions of the undergraduate and graduate course offerings at a number of the elite Eastern universities, which in years past paid little or no attention to Black Americans. The change that has been wrought in a generation is quite astonishing.

At Harvard, for example, I found no fewer than a dozen English Department courses in which the writings of Black authors are prominently featured. Two of these, to be sure, are taught by Henry Louis Gates, Jr., who chairs the Afro-American Studies Department as well as holding a position in the English Department. But the presence of Black authors in exclusively English Department courses is striking, nonetheless. A course on American Autobiography lists among the authors to be read Frederick Douglass, Olaudah Equiano, Harriet Jacobs, Malcolm X, and Zora Neale Hurston. Hurston shows up as well in a course on Language and Culture in American Modernism, and is the especial focus of a course on Southern Folklore and Southern Literature. Jacobs and Douglass turn up again, and Toni Morrison and Ralph Ellison make an appearance. An undergraduate course on Fiction Writing is taught by Jamaica Kincaid, a prominent Black author.

Even the Harvard History Department, famous in the past as a redoubt of self-congratulatory, inward-looking, old-fashioned panjundrums of the historical profession, sports eighteen courses in which explicit attention is paid to the experiences of African Americans. There is, of course, no telling from course titles how the materials are actually taught—two of the eighteen are taught by Stephen Thernstrom, who with his wife Abigail has made a name for himself as a foe of affirmative action, multi-culturalism, and other such heresies. But Thernstrom is a good social historian, despite the direction of his sentiments, and it seems clear from the array of course offerings that a student wanting to learn about the place of African Americans in American history can pretty well fill up his or her program with the History Department courses.

I found the same Black presence in the course offerings at Princeton and Yale. I don't think we need to carry out an extensive survey of college and university catalogues to be confident that for the present, the major authors of the Afro-American literary tradition will be accorded their place on the reading lists distributed to students at the beginning of each college semester, and a pretty good sprinkling of minor authors will receive some notice as well.

To be sure, there will always be fads and fashions in the life of the mind, and this author or that will at one time be widely read, at another time ignored. When I was a young philosophy student, no one paid any attention to Emerson and Thoreau, who were thought to be lightweight essayists. Now, it seems, they are all the rage, and deep thinkers take them seriously. It is hard for us to remember that in the eighteenth century, Plato and Aristotle were in eclipse, and Cicero, who has always seemed to me to be a third-rate imitator at best, was held in the highest esteem. Difficult as it may be for young literature students to believe, Melville was paid very little attention by the academic community until the Harvard critic F. O. Matthiessen succeeded in rehabilitating him. Even Shakespeare has had his good and bad centuries. So the fortunes of Hurston, Wright, Baldwin, and Ellison will undoubtedly wax and wane.

In the field of history, the situation is, if anything, even better. Thomas Bailey's expression of anxiety for the historical reputations of "significant white men" is simply unimaginable at a meeting of the Organization of American Historians today. Many of the most brilliant and most widely read American historians these days, White *and* Black, are students of the history of slavery and its aftermath. The scholarly journals are filled with investigations of every conceivable aspect of the lives and experiences of Black Americans. Things have been tough in the Academy lately for those with doctorates in the Humanities, but making some aspect of Black Studies your specialty these days actually improves rather than hurts your chances of getting a teaching job.

For the moment the battle of inclusion has been won. But I am painfully aware that the struggle for racial justice and for the simplest acknowledgment of the humanity of African Americans is by no means a story of steady progress. We have seen other times in the history of America when it looked as though genuine racial victories were being won, and gains made permanent, only to have a reaction set in that snatched all or most of those gains away. Indeed, we are in such a period of retreat at this moment. It remains to be seen whether the victories of inclusion in college curricula are sustained or reversed in the next third of a century.

A second component of the original program for a recognition of the Black experience was the call for scholarly studies of the history, literature, and culture of the peoples of sub-Saharan Africa. European and American anthropologists had, of course, for some time been producing ethnographic accounts of supposedly primitive peoples in Africa and elsewhere— "primitive" in this context usually meaning lacking in atomic weapons and tending to wear fewer clothes than are required by northern climates. But despite the efforts of a number of distinguished students of Africa, White and Black, the demand for scholarly recognition of sub-Saharan Africa ran into extraordinary opposition.

You would have thought this one was a no-brainer. After all, in the 1960s, thanks to the Cold War, the federal government was funding all manner of area studies programs as well as the study of potentially strategic languages. Russian Research Institutes, Eastern European Area Programs, Asian Studies Centers, Latin American Studies Certificate Programs—all were the recipients of government money. Who could possibly object to a study of the history, languages, literatures, and cultures of African peoples?

The problem was that for more than a century it had been a tenet of faith among Western intellectuals that sub-Saharan Africa does not *have* a history, a literature, or a culture worthy of study by anyone other than an anthropologist. The *locus classicus* for this bizarre and demeaning view is Hegel's *Lectures on the Philosophy of History*, delivered for the first time in 1822. Hegel's dismissive discussion of Africa has been quoted many times, but it is worth quoting again. I urge the reader who is not Black to try to imagine how it feels to hear, from the man widely thought to be the greatest thinker of the past two centuries, that one has no history and hence counts for nothing in the larger scheme of things.

In the Introduction to the *Lectures*, Hegel turns his attention momentarily to Africa [excluding Egypt]. The following passages give the flavor of his remarks:

> Africa proper, as far as History goes back, has remained—for all purposes of connection with the rest of the world—shut up; it is the Gold-land compressed within itself—the land of childhood, which lying beyond the day of self-conscious history, is enveloped in the dark mantle of Night. . . . The peculiarly African character is difficult to comprehend, for the very reason that in reference to it, we must quite give up the principle which naturally accompanies all *our* ideas—the category of Universality. In Negro life the characteristic point is the fact that consciousness has not yet attained to the realization of any substantial objective existence—as for example, God, or

Law—in which the interest of man's volition is involved and in which he realizes his own being [*and so on, for several pages*].

At this point we leave Africa, not to mention it again. For it is in no historical part of the world; it has no movement or development to exhibit. . . . What we properly understand by Africa, is the Unhistorical, Undeveloped Spirit, still involved in the conditions of mere nature, and which had to be presented here only as on the threshold of the World's History.

It is astonishing how influential these words have been, both in creating and in validating the Euro-American fantasy of "the Dark Continent." The central theme of Hegel's remarks is the *ahistoricity* of Africa. Hegel claims that unlike Europe, Asia, the Indian subcontinent, or even the New World, sub-Saharan Africa lives in a timeless present. Nothing ever *happens* there, save the endless succession of seasons and generations. This is the underlying myth that for generations sustained ethnographers in their quixotic search for "primitive peoples"—peoples, that is to say, who, though alive today, are nevertheless living prehistoric lives. Quite sophisticated social scientists, capable of the most nuanced methodological meditations, have built their entire research programs on this curious fantasy.

The same fantasy crops up in such popular entertainments as the African safari movie—*King Solomon's Mines* is perhaps the greatest of the genre. These movies always begin in a safe, comfortable world, socially and physically secure, like a Victorian drawing room.

The principal characters undertake a dangerous journey to "darkest Africa," in search of a loved one, lost treasure, or the origins of the Nile River. At first the journey is easy—carriage, train, ocean liner—but once they get to Africa, the trip gets progressively more difficult. The heroes and heroines plunge into impassable jungle, they struggle across trackless wastes, they nearly die of thirst and snake bite, their native bearers run away, frightened by sounds and warnings that do not, of course, rattle a European. Finally, near death, they stumble upon their quest—King Solomon's diamond mines, Lake Victoria, the bones of the lost loved one. Then begins the long trip home, each stage of which gets easier as they get closer to England. The last stages, like the first, are comfortable and familiar. They arrive, at last, back in the secure world they left.

These fictions are charming, but if one thinks about them even for a moment it is obvious that they make no sense at all. Darkest Africa, which is represented as virtually impassable, is, after all, the home of the "natives" whom the travelers meet along their way. Those "natives" are born there, they grow up there, they marry, have children, work, fight, engage in political activities, and in general do there all the same sorts of things that proper Englishmen do in London. Getting around that part of the world is as easy and natural—or as difficult and unnatural—to them as getting around London is to an Englishman. If Africa were as objectively inimical to human existence as the movie suggests, the local residents would long ago have died out.

To grasp the fantasied nature of the representation, just imagine the entire story from the point of view of an African, who leaves his comfortable, familiar world to venture in ever more difficult stages to bewildering, dangerous, impassable London, only to return finally to his safe, secure, familiar African village. To its great credit, the revisionist telling of the Tarzan story in the movie *Greystoke* captures this reversal rather well. For a truly sophisticated representation of the physical and social world from the perspective of at least some Africans, we must read the novels of the great Nigerian author, Chinua Achebe.

Lest one imagine that the myth of darkest Africa survives only in movies and reprints of Victorian fiction, let me draw once more on the researches of Lawrence Levine. With a scholarly reserve of which I fear I am not capable, Levine gently chastises a number of contemporary historians for

> an ungenerous defensiveness when the United States and Western civilization are compared to other cultures. [Levine writes:] African cultures, [Arthur] Schlesinger tells us, are based on "despotism, superstition, tribalism, and fanaticism." The "principal offerings" of "Central African culture," the philosopher Lewis S. Feuer wrote recently, have been "disease and massacre." Similarly, the celebrated historian Hugh Trevor-Roper, in defense of what he termed "Europacentric" history, advised those undergraduates who were asking for courses in African history that "there is none, or very little: there is only the history of the Europeans in Africa. The rest is largely darkness, like the history of pre-European, pre-Columbian America. And darkness is not a subject for history."

It is difficult to imagine prominent scholars being so willing to exhibit their ignorance with such bland self-confidence on any other topic. It is as though, when it comes to the doings of Black people, one need not bother even to exercise an elementary precaution against making a fool of oneself.

The exclusion of sub-Saharan Africa from world history has in recent decades been dealt a series of powerful blows by the work of a number of comparative historians drawing on the insights of Immanuel Wallerstein's theory of world systems. Once Arabic, Persian, Chinese, and other archival sources are added to the data derived from the European languages, a very different picture emerges of the economic, cultural, and political events of the thousand-year period from the rise of Islam to the sixteenth century.

Europe, Africa, the Near and Middle East, the Indian sub-continent, the Malay archipelago, and China turn out all to have been linked in a well-established network of trade routes organized around a number of nodal points. West Africa was both a source of such highly prized materials as gold and also a consumer of finished goods, in a complex multilateral trade. The African trade traveled northwards across the Sahara, west to the Atlantic, and east to the Indian ocean. At one moment in history, the taste of African rulers for a particular quality of fine blue-dyed wool cloth actually sparked an economic boomlet in the North of England, where the raw wool originated.

As for the notion that sub-Saharan Africa has no political history prior to the arrival of European imperial invaders and colonists, that too is simply an expression of ignorance, very much like the long-held belief, now happily given up, that Native Americans were utterly apolitical "savages" until blessed with the ministrations of the Pilgrim Fathers. Thanks to a number of television specials and movies and to the anti-apartheid struggle, Americans are somewhat more aware of the complex politics of the pre-European period in what is now South Africa. "Shaka Zulu" is not a household name, but save to the likes of Saul Bellow, his empire-building and military feats are part of the furniture of the well-stocked Euro-American mind. The equally impressive imperial dynasties of Zimbabwe and of West Africa are perhaps less well known, but there is really no excuse for statements like those of Schlesinger, Trever-Roper, and Feuer.

A variant of the call for African Studies has been the proposal to establish programs that study what is called the African Diaspora. In just the past year or two, the African American Studies Department at the University of California Berkeley has established a doctoral program in African Diaspora Studies, and the Yale University Afro-American Studies Department has adopted a similar perspective.

There are good historical and demographic grounds for taking the African Diaspora as a unit of study. As many as ninety percent of all the Africans seized and transported to the Western Hemisphere during the four centuries of the slave trade ended up in the Caribbean or Central and South America, not in the Northern Hemisphere. The actual volume of the slave trade has been difficult to pin down, with estimates ranging from ten to twenty-five million men, women, and children forcibly transported to the New World, but there is widespread agreement that only a small fraction of the captives were brought to North America.

To be sure, there is a rather odd problem conceptually with the notion of African Diaspora studies. The best archeological, paleontological, and genetic evidence has established decisively that the human species, *Homo sapiens sapiens*, appeared in its current genetic form in Africa somewhere between one hundred and two hundred thousand years ago, and then spread by a series of migrations across the entire globe. Thus *all* human beings are members of a diaspora originating in Africa, the only ground for distinction being a matter of when in the hundred millennia of our existence a particular dispersal took place. By the way, Europeans seem to have migrated out of Africa rather later than the peoples of the American continents.

Strictly speaking, therefore, the entire university curriculum should be gathered under the rubric "African Diaspora." But in this, as in so much else concerning human beings, the social, the cultural, and the conceptual trump the merely physical or natural. When the Berkeley Department of African American Studies announced a doctoral program in African Diaspora Studies, it probably did not have in mind the writings of Confucius, the rise of Christianity, the economy of ancient India, or the varieties of pre-Columbian art.

But neither African Studies nor Studies of the African Diaspora is the appropriate *locus* for the telling of the true American story, because although each of them has contributed to that story, neither focuses on *America*.

A more plausible candidate is the school of Black Studies that goes by the label *Afrocentricity*. These are scholars, led by Temple University professor Molefi Asante, who claim to tell the story of African Americans, *but from the perspective of Africa*. In the past thirty years, Afrocentricity has been the most influential and the most controversial of the intellectual enterprises that have called themselves Black Studies or Afro-American Studies. Asante established the very first doctoral program in Afro-American Studies at Temple, and the students who have come through that program now teach across the country in a great many Afro-American Studies departments. Asante's ideas deserve a good deal of careful attention.

Molefi Asante and his followers, like the old radio character The Shadow [Lamont Cranston], seem to have the power to cloud White men's minds. My informal survey of the flood of anti-Black Studies screeds, tracts, and diatribes suggests that as much as nine-tenths of it is triggered by Asante's Afrocentrism.

As we might expect, Arthur Schlesinger, Jr. grows rather apoplectic at the thought of Afrocentrism, and apparently considers it a major threat to Western Civilization and The American Dream. In *The Disuniting of America*, Schlesinger devotes a good deal of space to Afrocentrism, particularly as it has affected the formulation of school curricula. Schlesinger is enamored of the Melting Pot myth of immigrant incorporation into American society, despite the fact that it has long since been debunked, and he *views with alarm* the impact of Afrocentrism on the health of the society.

> I am constrained to feel [he writes somewhat disingenuously—since he seems thoroughly inclined to believe what he is supposedly being compelled to accept] that the cult of ethnicity in general and the Afrocentric campaign in particular do not bode well either for American education or for the future of the minorities.

Leaving to one side the question whether "the minorities" either want or need Schlesinger's solicitude, or indeed can stomach it, I confess that it is a constant astonishment to me that scholars of his bent can write this way without so much as a flicker of recognition that the texts and stories they ingested as students and have regurgitated as professors are themselves also celebrations of a cult of ethnicity—the ethnicity of the Northern European settlers.

One final word about Schlesinger. Speaking of the emphasis on Africa, and comparing it with, among other things, American Jews' pride in the doings of Israel, he writes:

> The glorification of the African past was accompanied by a campaign to replace Anglo "slave" names with African names, to wear African costumes, to replicate African rituals. LeRoi Jones, who had said in 1962 that "history for the Negro, before America, must remain an emotional abstraction," now saw Africa more concretely and changed his name to Amiri Baraka. Arthur Smith became Molefi Kete Asante and called on others to embrace African names.

The sneering condescension in this passage is astonishing in a man who, if nothing else, has led a cosmopolitan life in the academy and in government. The scare quotes around the word *slave* perfectly encapsulate Schlesinger's moral perspective. Does he think that "LeRoi Jones" and "Arthur Smith" are the names these men would have borne had their ancestors not been seized and enslaved? Does Schlesinger, an American historian after all, know nothing about the origins of the names of the descendants of slaves? How much more nuanced and thoughtful it might have been for him to draw a comparison with names like Schwartz, Applebaum, Ornstein, Schneider, and Weiss, which are German names thrust on Jews forced to live under oppressive regimes. If Mr. Schneider can become Mr. Taylor when he emigrates to America, and Schwartz and Weiss can become Black and White, why cannot Arthur Smith become Molefi Asante? Perhaps Arthur Smith found it more difficult to melt in the great American pot because neither he nor his ancestors chose to come here and because, name change or no, he would immediately be recognized as a descendant of slaves.

What *is* Afrocentrism or Afrocentricity, according to Asante? It is, to put it as simply as possible, a theory of language, of the oral traditions of rhetoric and discourse rooted in African culture, through which we can, Asante tells us, arrive at a non-Eurocentric understanding of human beings and human culture. *Afrocentricity*, he says, is

> the most complete philosophical totalization of the African being-at-the-center of his or her existence. It is not merely an artistic or literary movement. Not only is it an individual or collective quest for authenticity, but it is above all the total use of method to effect psychological, political, social, cultural, and economic change. The Afrocentric idea is beyond decolonizing the mind.

Asante was trained in the field of Communications Studies, and his concern with the technical terms and problems of that subject are apparent throughout his writings. He places great emphasis on the oral traditions of African culture, and on the interactions between speaker and audience that are central to such traditions, using his own term, "orature," as a general category for those practices and traditions. He also traces the impact of this orature on the oral conventions of African Americans, drawing examples from sermons, public speaking, rapping, signifying, and other language games and arts.

But although Asante's primary focus is on linguistic structures, practices, and traditions, he is always reaching for something more—for the essential understanding of the human condition that he believes can be found in African and Afro-American language. He has a vision of a harmonious human society in which language mediates a union of feeling, thought, and action within and between members of a community. He finds this harmony present in African traditional societies and their linguistic practices, and markedly absent from what he sees as mechanical, linear, individualistic, isolating tendencies in European/White American linguistic and social traditions.

Asante is extremely critical of the parochialism of Euro-American social, literary, and ideological theorists, and repeatedly declares his intention to free himself from the limitations of that intellectual tradition. Some of his most telling thrusts are directed at such figures as Paul de Man, Jacques Derrida, Jürgen Habermas, Theodor Adorno, Max Horkheimer, Herbert Marcuse, Northrop Frye, and Ferdinand de Saussure. "The preponderant Eurocentric myths of universalism, objectivity, and classical traditions," he claims, "retain a provincial European cast."

Sometimes, Asante adopts what seems to me to be a rather modest and easily defensible stance, as when he defines Afrocentricity as "placing African ideals at the center of any analysis that involves African culture and behavior." At other times, he offers a more expansive view of Afrocentricity, as a method of understanding and a conception of language that is superior to, and hence presumably ought to displace, European/American methods and conceptions. In either case, he offers Afrocentric methods of speech and analysis as an antidote to the oppressive, colonizing infliction of a Eurocentric mind set on Africans and their descendants in the diaspora.

To these themes and arguments, Asante now adds another element, at once more dramatic and vastly more controversial. Directly rebutting Hegel's disparaging dismissal of Africa as a land without history, reason, or culture, Asante lays claim in the name of all persons of African descent to the greatest of all the ancient traditions, those of Egypt, or Kemet. ("Kemet" is the name sometimes used to refer to ancient or classical Egypt, and Asante, like Maulana Karenga and others, prefers it to "Egypt.")

> The Afrocentric analysis [he says,] re-establishes the centrality of the ancient Kemetic (Egyptian) civilization and the Nile Valley cultural complex as points of reference for an African perspective in much the same way as Greece and Rome serve as reference points for the European world.

Asante makes a good deal of supposed correspondences between Egyptian hieroglyphs and the signs or symbols in sub-Saharan African languages for the same words as evidence of a linguistic influence. He also writes at length about the characteristics of ancient Egyptian culture and society as a paradigm that can stand as an alternative—equally valuable and indisputably older—to the oft invoked paradigms of Classical Greek and Roman culture. As one might expect, he emphasizes the primacy of Egypt in inventing or propagating a variety of religious, mathematical, scientific, and philosophical ideas, and calls attention to the fact that Egypt powerfully influenced Greece, *not* the other way around.

Finally, and perhaps most controversially, Asante argues that African *Americans* should look to this Kemetic tradition for their roots, for inspiration, for whatever it is that modern Europeans and White Americans can hope to derive from Classical Greece and Rome. It is this proposal to substitute an African cultural orientation for the present emphasis on Classical Greece and Rome in school curricula that drives critics wild.

It is a fair bet that had Asante confined himself to a call for grounding the study of *Africa* in African culture and history, he would have stirred up much less fuss, although even in so narrowly constrained a form the proposal would certainly have triggered some anguished cries of obscurantism and fears of danger to the great traditions of Western Civilization. But in putting forward his conception of Kemetic tradition as a competitor to, indeed as superior to, the traditions of Western Civilization, and in calling on African Americans to embrace Kemet rather than Greece and Rome, Asante has definitively placed himself outside of, and against, the White intellectual and cultural mainstream—as indeed he intended to do.

Now, I don't really think there is much merit in Asante's project. And I certainly do not think it can serve as the theoretical grounding for the true American story. *But all the conceptual and methodological weaknesses in his project can be found, in exactly the same form, in the mainstream, valorized project associated with such Euro-American thinkers as Hegel, Herder, Heidegger, Arendt, Barzun, and Bloom [Allan, not Harold].*

Let me say that again another way, because it is liable to come as a bit of a shock to sophisticated readers who may even have been agreeing with me thus far. *Methodologically speaking, there is no difference between Asante's celebration of ancient Egypt as the source of a great African cultural tradition, and the celebration of Greece and Rome as the source of a great Euro-American tradition. Both are simply myths of a Golden Past, myths of a special time and place at which civilization begins, and to which all subsequent thought and culture must be oriented.*

The celebration of what is rather oddly called "Western Civilization" has become such a staple of the intellectual, political, and cultural life of

Europeans and Americans—and also, of course, so central a tenet of the rationalization of modern Euro-American imperial adventures—that it will strike many readers as simply bizarre or insulting to equate the glorious story of Judeo-Christian-Graeco-Roman civilization with Asante's African fantasies. Surely political correctness has its limits! But if we steel ourselves for a moment to the seductions of Western Civ, as it has come to be known on college campuses, we will not find it difficult to see the parallels with Asante's project.

Consider, for example, the thought of the philosopher and political theorist Hannah Arendt, widely esteemed in Europe and America as among the deepest, most sophisticated, most penetrating minds of the twentieth century. Arendt, like so many learned thinkers of the Western tradition, represents the cultural and political history of the last two and a half millennia of the European peninsula of Eurasia as a tragic story of decline from former glory. Her narrative perspective is that of a cultivated and alienated member of the continental upper middle classes, and the dominant tonality is nostalgia for the lost glories of Classical Athens.

Fifth- and Fourth-Century BC Athens occupy a privileged position in the fiction conjured by Arendt. Their invocation consequently carries a moral and aesthetic weight in her discourse utterly incompatible with the historical actuality. A cluster of small agricultural and trading communities in the Eastern Mediterranean with a relatively undeveloped technology is accorded by Arendt a heightened resonance and importance, in much the same way that communicants of other faiths bend the knee to Calvary in the first century of this era, or to Paris in the 1790s, St. Petersburg in October 1917, and the Constitutional Convention in Philadelphia in 1787.

This is not to suggest that Arendt's account of ancient Greece is factually inaccurate, any more than to suggest that Tolstoy got the facts of the Battle of Borodino wrong in *War and Peace*. An historical novel written with meticulous attention to the latest historical scholarship is no less a fiction for all the learning of its author.

Because Arendt writes from within a fictional world in which ancient Greece shines as the golden age toward which we longingly yearn, rather than from within the real world in which the affairs of fifth century BC Greece are merely one among many examples of human collective behavior—because she, like so many of the most distinguished intellectuals of Europe and America, persistently confuses the two in her writings—it is almost impossible to come to grips realistically and objectively with her theses, any more than it is possible from within Asante's fantasy to engage in a scholarly fashion with his yearning for the glories that were Kemet.

The common failing of Arendt and Asante—and of countless other celebrators of cultural glories—is their tendency to understand human history as a timeless accumulation of artistic, philosophical, and religious ideas, rather than as the temporal unfolding of collective struggles to produce the means of existence and to control both the product and the process by which it is produced. In short, Arendt, Asante, and their sort are historical Idealists. Like Hegel before them, they imagine that philosophical ideas, not material realities, are the principal movers of history. The exaltation of the Great Books of Western Civilization—or of Kemetic Civilization—is simply the curricular embodiment of this discredited supposition.

It is not the way in which Asante carries out his project that is at fault, nor is it the fact that he seeks to elevate Africa above Europe, though that is certainly what brings down such opprobrium on his head. It is rather that *both* his project *and* the widely endorsed and praised effort to articulate the central defining characteristics of Western Civilization start from Idealist premises that are simply philosophically untenable. It is surely a bitter irony that Asante, outraged by Hegel's contemptuous dismissal of "the dark continent," has produced what can only be called a Hegelian theory of Afrocentricity.

Who can offer a home to the American Griot? Not a department devoted to Africana Studies, or a Department devoted to a study of the African Diaspora, for their focus is not on America—they do not seek to tell the story of America. Nor can a department devoted to Cultural Studies, such as that of Molefi Asante, serve as the appropriate home for our story-teller, for the premise of Cultural Studies is that each racial, ethnic, national, or linguistic group has its own story—all of them equally valuable, but none of them *the story of America*.

Only a department devoted to the study of the African-*American* experience can serve as the home for the new American Griot. Because of the centrality in the American story of the role of African Americans, a consideration of the Afro-American experience is nothing less than a *reconsideration* of America. Through the prism of Afro-American Studies, the light shining from the City upon a Hill is fractured into the rainbow of the composite American experience. When that light is resynthesized, we are presented with a new image of America, an image critical as well as celebratory. Afro-American Studies is not the Negro Quarter in the ghetto of Multiculturalism—a vibrant place of strange sounds and smells that the uptown folks can visit on a night out. Afro-American Studies is the necessary corrective to a four-centuries-long misappropriation of the American experience.

But why an academic *department* of Afro-American Studies? Why not rely on the new Master Narrative of the American Story to be told by scholars, poets, novelists, and public figures wherever they are situated? The story I have told in this book was taught to me by many people, some in my own department, some in other Afro-American Studies departments, but most of them not in such departments at all. Leon Litwack, Lawrence Levine, Jacqueline Jones, and Charles Joyner are all historians. Leon Higgenbotham taught law when he was not serving as a Federal Appeals Court Judge. Vincent Harding taught at a school of theology. The great W. E. B. Du Bois did not live quite long enough ever to see the creation of a department of Afro-American Studies.

Nell Painter is a distinguished historian who has served two terms as head of the Princeton University Black Studies program. In an essay for the *Chronicle of Higher Education*, she spoke of some of the reasons why we need strong Black Studies programs:

> To attract and keep black faculty members, an institution needs to have a critical mass of black students and faculty members. Black students and faculty members and black studies flourish in good company and wither in isolation.

No matter how many victories are won, the attacks on the legitimacy of Black Studies continue.

> So where are we 30 years later? [she asks]. Utterly exhausted! . . . It seems like every single change has required struggle, and no improvement becomes permanent. I wonder whether that will always be true.

The Importance of Being a Department

In order to see why it is so important that there be strong, well-established academic departments of Afro-American Studies, we need to look for a bit at the inner workings of universities. Now this is not a subject that brings delight to the soul, even for members of the academy. But it is in the bureaucratic structure of the university that power is secreted, not in its flowery mission statements or Commencement Day ceremonies.

Once again, let me begin with a story. When I entered Harvard College as a young Freshman fifty-four years ago, the College was just phasing in a new undergraduate curriculum called General Education. There was nothing fancy about Gen Ed, as it very quickly came to be known. It consisted of a number of large lecture courses in the Humanities, the Social Sciences, and the Natural Sciences, taught in many cases by the most senior and distinguished members of the faculty. Each undergraduate, as part of his year-long courses [Harvard was all-male in those days], was required to take one course in each category. My freshman year, I took a marvelous course with a fiery red-haired historian named Sam Beer. We studied everything from the Anglo-Saxon wergeld to the fall of the Weimar Republic.

Because these courses were required of all students, and also because they were among the best courses in the catalogue, Gen Ed very quickly became a fixture at Harvard. By the time it was my turn to teach in the program eight years later, it seemed to undergraduates as though Gen Ed had existed forever, and would go on existing forever.

But there was no *department* of General Education. There was a committee of senior faculty who administered the program, recruiting professors to teach the courses, choosing which courses to offer, and approving a small number of "upper level Gen Ed" courses which were simply exciting interdisciplinary offerings that someone wanted to teach. Nor was there a *faculty* of General Education. To be sure, a great many young men [and a few young women] were appointed to Instructorships or Assistant Professorships in General Education *and* something or other—my official title during my three-year stay in the program was Instructor in General Education and Philosophy. But we all understood that it was impossible to get tenure in Gen Ed. For us, it was a very pleasant professional dead end.

Years passed—indeed, decades passed—and finally the Harvard faculty grew weary of General Education. At first, it had been marvelous for senior professors to create broad-scale courses drawing on the widest possible range of materials, which they could lay before three or four hundred adoring undergraduates. But as Max Weber pointed out so long ago, even charisma becomes routinized, and eventually the task of teaching Gen Ed courses was handed off to junior faculty.

So one day—so to speak—the Faculty of Arts and Sciences voted to end General Education, and replace it with something new. There is nothing surprising about this turn of events. Faculties are constantly reshuffling their teaching materials, reconfiguring what they require of undergraduates, creating new courses, new mixes. It keeps all of us young and limber, mentally speaking. But there is a lesson to be learned from it.

Programs and requirements that seem eternal to undergraduates may be passing fancies from the perspective of the faculty. Undergraduates, after all, are like mayflies. Their entire life span is only four years, which is not even one sabbatical cycle for a professor. In the glacial world of the academy, four years is merely a Spring. Even though General Education lasted at Harvard for thirty years or more, no one ever got tenure in it, no one ever earned a degree in it, and today it is remembered only by people like myself, old enough to tell stories of their youth.

And General Education was not especially controversial. There were no alumni revolts against it. Officials of the Federal Government did not inveigh against it. It did not even generate much opposition from old guard faculty, as educational innovations so often do. Harvard just tired of it, and decided to replace it with something new.

Think now of Black Studies. It was born in turmoil out of struggle and rage. It provoked from the very first moment of its existence the most violent and intemperate opposition. Virtually every college or university administration that agreed to the establishment of a Black Studies program did so for nakedly political reasons—to avoid campus revolts, to end a building seizure, as a response to the threat of violence. Black Studies did not emerge from faculty committees calmly reflecting on the life of the mind and concluding that the curriculum needed to be enriched by the Black experience. Even the most publicly progressive of academic administrations wanted no more than a token Black presence on their campuses, until forced by the larger events of the nation to open their doors a bit wider.

So it is that when Black Studies programs came into existence, the White campuses on which they were housed used every device to make sure that they could be terminated, when things calmed down, without breaking tenure or disrupting the bureaucratic administration of the institution.

The simplest device was the faculty committee—the arrangement that served Harvard so well during the life of General Education. To an undergraduate who finds a Committee on Black Studies in operation when he or she arrives on the campus, and sees it still functioning four years later, Black Studies looks like a permanent fixture. But to senior faculty and administrators, it is transparently a temporary arrangement. A Committee can be disbanded simply by a memorandum.

The appointment of junior faculty gives a somewhat more settled appearance to Black Studies, even though the positions may not be, as we say in the trade, tenure track. Outsiders may have a hard time distinguishing between graduate student teaching assistants and professors, let alone between tenure track, non-tenure track, and tenured professors, but to the faculty, whose bread and butter depends on these distinctions, there is no confusion. A university can quite easily hire a whole raft of junior non-tenure track Black Studies assistant professors without making the slightest permanent commitment either to them or to their field.

Equally meretricious, though considerably more impressive looking, is the practice of joint appointments. At the non-tenured level, these appointments are a snare and a delusion. The junior professor in, let us say, History and Afro-American Studies, must somehow ingratiate herself both with the senior members of the History department, who care only about her performance as an historian and give her no credit for her contributions to Black Studies, and with the members of the committee administering the Afro-American Studies degree, who come from many departments and neither see nor credit her services to History. What is more, almost certainly a majority of the senior members of the History department will be unsympathetic with Black Studies in general, and unwilling to commit one of their scarce tenure slots to someone who is, in their eyes, not *really* an historian.

Even when politically charged issues are not involved, junior faculty find it forbiddingly difficult to negotiate these rapids. When one adds race to the mix, it becomes nearly impossible. Finally, there is the device of joint tenured appointments. In a university with a strong tradition of faculty tenure, this arrangement has the very great virtue of protecting Black Studies professors from losing their jobs. But although it protects the professors, it does not protect the field of Black Studies. When the turmoil quiets down, when intellectual currents change direction, when a star professor leaves for a gig somewhere else, or when America goes into a period of reactionary retreat on matters of race—which it does with great regularity—Black Studies as an academic field can be terminated at the university, and the faculty distributed to their home departments. After all, the senior professors who taught General Education had tenure. That did not protect General Education from being ended when fashions changed.

At the moment, the highest profile Black Studies department in the country is the Harvard department led by Henry Louis Gates, Jr. The Harvard department has garnered so much media coverage that the educated White world is quite aware of the Dream Team of distinguished and well-known professors who were gathered there by Gates. Cornell West, William Julius Wilson, Anthony Appiah, Evelyn Higgenbotham—that is a line-up to make a Dean's heart swell with pride. To the undergraduates at Harvard, it must seem that Afro-American Studies is as permanent as the marble of Widener Library. Nothing, surely, can threaten its continued existence.

And yet—*every single senior and junior professor in the department was hired on a joint appointment*—Gates as a member of the English Department, West in the theology faculty, Wilson on the faculty of the Kennedy School of Government, Appiah as a member of the Philosophy Department. Speaking strictly from a purely bureaucratic point of view, *there is no Harvard department of Afro-American Studies*. Harvard could terminate it tomorrow, and simply redistribute the faculty to their *real* academic homes.

But surely that will not happen! At this moment, Skip Gates and his Dream Team are the biggest thing happening at Harvard. Gates has raised a vast sum of money, and has made himself far and away the best known Black intellectual in the White community. Harvard gives every evidence of being deeply committed to Afro-American Studies.

No doubt. As they were to General Education. But what would happen if Gates were to move on to head up a great foundation or run a major university or even—in different times—to a position in the Federal Government? Cornell West and Anthony Appiah have already been wooed away by Princeton, and Harvard's new president, Lawrence Summers, has made it clear that he does not share his predecessor's enthusiasm for Black Studies. What then is the future of Afro-American Studies at Harvard? It almost died once, after all.

No, in the Byzantine world of the academy, there is only one solid foundation on which to build a discipline: A stand-alone regular academic department with a regular budget lodged in a faculty overseen by a Dean and staffed by a full complement of senior professors who have tenure solely and entirely in that department. Physics would not accept less. Neither would History, Mathematics, or Sociology. Why should Black Studies?

University departments have been around for such a long time that even senior tenured faculty tend to consider them as eternal, but in the life of the academy—which, after all, traces itself back two and a half millennia to Plato's Groves of Academe—they too are a very recent phenomenon. Recall T. H. White's lovely conceit in *The Sword in the Stone*, in which he has Merlin change the young Arthur into all manner of animals, vegetables, and minerals so that he will have a deep understanding of the natural world before assuming his kingship. At one point, Wart becomes a mountain, and discovers how slowly the world changes from its perspective. We need something like Merlin's trick to see the university department in its true light.

In the Middle Ages, universities were itinerant communities of scholars. Later on, they organized themselves into faculties—of law, of medicine, of theology. When the nineteenth century German institution of the research university was transplanted in America, the faculty at first consisted of a constellation of professors, surrounded by clouds of lesser beings who handled some of the teaching chores. That then changed. As Alain Touraine tells us in his valuable study of the American academic system, "the great American innovation was the creation of departments. They made their appearance at Cornell and Johns Hopkins as early as 1880, at Harvard and Chicago around 1881–82, and at Columbia in the late nineties."

The department was not at first a locus of tenure, for nothing like tenure existed in the eighteen-nineties. The idea of job security as a protection of academic freedom arose during the political assaults on professors triggered by the hysteria of the First World War, and it was not until after the Second World War that the modern protection of tenure became widespread in the academy. By the time Black Studies was launched, however, it had become the settled practice of virtually all American colleges and universities to grant tenure to faculty after a lengthy probationary period and a searching professional review. The practice was adopted throughout the academy of awarding tenure only to regular members of academic departments. Teaching positions were regularly advertised as "tenure track" or "non-tenure track," and only those on tenure track appointments were even eligible to be considered for promotion with tenure.

There is no way of knowing how long the present system of departments and tenure will last. Tenure was bitterly resisted by administrators and trustees when it was first proposed, and has been fought ever since. University administrations are constantly searching for ways to overcome the stubborn independence of professors. Breaking up departments in the name of innovation, or interdisciplinarity, or pedagogical improvement will always appeal to provosts, presidents, and trustees who are prone to the occupational delusion that they are the university. But for so long as departments are the vehicle for the reproduction of disciplines and the protection of the intellectual freedom of professors, Black Studies must demand full independent departmental status in the college or university.

Here, then, is my answer to the question, Who shall guard and tell the new Master Narrative for America? The American Griots must have a home in university Black Studies departments that take as their focus the African-*American* experience—departments that seek to understand America as a whole through the lens of the African-American experience.

A CONCLUDING WORD

And so, having set out on a long journey, I have, like Kierkegaard's Christian, arrived where I began. Or so it may seem. In truth, nothing about my understanding of my country is the same, nor can it ever be again. Gone forever is the illusion that America was founded as a haven for those seeking freedom, and has remained since a city upon a hill, shining like a beacon and holding out the hope that in this exceptional land, the founding dream will slowly be realized.

In place of this fantasy is the realization that North America, like Australia, South Africa, India, and many other lands, has for the past four centuries been a White Settler state, where the Racial Contract, in Charles Mills's evocative phrase, is imposed on the backs of those whose skins are not classified as "white." America is and has since the seventeenth century been a land of Bondage and Freedom—Bondage for the many, and then for those not White, Freedom for the few, and then for those who are White.

This realization is not an expression of cynicism or pessimism, as some might imagine, for to be cynical, one must suppose that an ideal is being honored only in the breach, and to be pessimistic, one must have lost hope that an ideal will be actualized. But the Ideal of Freedom has never been the story of America. From the first, White settlers sought to exploit the land and its resources by means of bound labor. Very quickly, they imposed on this effort a racial coding that continues, in one form or another, to the present day. The population of our prisons testifies to this; so do the profiling practices of our police, the decisions of our Supreme Court, the statistical picture of the distribution of wealth and income, and our popular culture.

Incurable optimist that I am, I prefer to see this refashioning of the American story as a first step toward the crafting of a truly liberatory project. All the major improvements in the condition of Black people in America have taken place either with their active and essential involvement, as in the Civil War, or under their leadership, as in the Civil Rights

Movement. But because we Whites remain in the majority, and control the levers of wealth and power, our illusions about the nature of America and our resistance to acknowledging the realities of race erect a formidable barrier to change.

Just as my role in the UMass Afro-American Studies Department has perforce been limited to that of *Shabbes goy*, doing a variety of useful but tiresome jobs, so my role in the struggle for racial justice must be secondary and supportive. My colleagues, and their brothers and sisters across America, will lead the next movement for racial justice, as they did the last one thirty and more years ago. I will be content if this little essay can guide some of my readers along the path I have taken.

I began with an observation by Kierkegaard, and perhaps I can end the same way. In the Preface to one of his shortest but most powerful works, the *Philosophical Fragments*, he mocks the followers of Hegel who constructed elaborate systems of philosophy and announced inflated claims for their writings. Forswearing all such pretensions, Kierkegaard writes,

> May I escape the tragicomic predicament of being forced to laugh at my own misfortune, as must have been the case with the poor people of Frederica, when they awoke one morning to read in the newspaper an account of a fire in their town, in which it was described how "the drums beat the alarm, the fire-engines rushed through the streets"—although the town of Frederica boasts only one fire-engine and not much more than one street; leaving it to be inferred that this one engine instead of making for the scene of the fire, took time to execute important maneuvers and flanking movements up and down the street.

I make no inflated claims for this little essay. It is not a new theory of Freedom, or of America. It offers no new facts, and scarcely any new thoughts. But it is an honest account of what I have learned during my twelve years as a White philosopher in an Afro-American Studies Department. As Kierkegaard says, I hope it will be accepted *proprio Marte, propriis auspiciis, proprio stipendio* (on its own errand, under its own auspices, for its own sake).

NOTES

Chapter Two

Page 32: Rather than tell the story of America in my words alone . . . In preparing to write this chapter, I was offered the opportunity to examine all eleven editions of Bailey's book by Ms. Padge Jordan of Houghton Mifflin, who not only pulled the books from the archives, but also provided me with a lovely corner office on the sixth floor of the Houghton Mifflin Building in downtown Boston, and with the use of a balky but manageable xerox machine. I am extremely grateful to her and to Houghton Mifflin for their cooperation.

Page 34: "America emerged . . ." Nevins and Commager, *America: The Story of a Free People*, 1st ed. (Oxford: At the Clarendon Press, 1942), v–vi.

Page 35: "The American Republic, which is still relatively . . ." Thomas A. Bailey, *The American Pageant*, (Boston: D. C. Heath, 1956), 4.

Page 35: "For we must consider . . ." John Winthrop, *Life and Letters of John Winthrop*, ed. Robert C. Winthrop, 2 vols. (New York: Da Capo Press, 1971), 19

Page 36: "Thus, out of the welter . . ." Samuel Eliot Morison and Henry Steele Commager, *The Growth of the American Republic*, 3rd ed. (New York: Oxford University Press, 1942), 36. This passage is added in the third edition, which was considerably enlarged.

Page 36: "The history of English settlement . . ." Nevins and Commager, *America*, 1st ed. (1942), 1.

Page 37: "There comes a time . . ." Morison and Commager, *The Growth of the American Republic*, 2nd ed. (New York: Oxford University Press, 1937), 162–63. [Added in the 2nd edition, which was enlarged to cover the period before 1763.]

Page 38: "One was the arrival . . ." Nevins and Commager, *America*, 1st ed. (1942), 6.

Page 38: "In 1619—a fateful date . . ." Bailey, *American Pageant*, 15.

Page 38: "A careful reading of . . ." Morison and Commager, 2nd ed. (1937), 166. [Added in the second edition as part of a longer passage criticizing recent historical works for reading their authors' political views back into the past.]

Page 38: "America was very fortunate . . ." Morison and Commager, *The Growth of the American Republic*, 1st ed. (New York: Oxford University Press, 1930), 167.

Page 39: "Sectional jealousy also raised . . ." Bailey, *American Pageant*, 141.

Page 39: "Sojourner Truth, who has become . . ." See Nell Irvin Painter, *Sojourner Truth: A Life, A Symbol* (New York: W. W. Norton, 1996), chapters 2 and 3.

Page 40: "As for Sambo," Morison and Commager, *Growth of the American Republic*, 1st ed. (1930), 415.

Page 41: "Topsy and Tom Sawyer's . . ." Ibid.

Page 41: "While the average Englishman . . ." Ibid., 416.

Page 41: "Flogging with the rawhide . . ." Ibid., 417.

Page 41: "If we overlook . . ." Ibid., 418.

Page 42: "Every Christmas molasses . . ." and subsequent passages. Nevins and Commager, *America*, 1st ed. (1942), 183–84.

Page 42: Thomas Bailey presents from the first . . . See Bailey, *American Pageant*, 358–66, passim.

Page 44: Even moderate abolitionism . . . See ibid., 367. I arrive at this figure by measuring with my ruler the diagram that Bailey himself calls a "rough approximation." For the remainder of the Bailey's discussion of the abolitionists, see pp. 367–73, passim.

Page 46: "The causes of secession . . ." Morison and Commager, *Growth of the American Republic*, 1st ed., 511–12.

Page 46: "To the hideous end . . ." Bailey, *American Pageant*, 450.

Page 47: "The American Negroes are the only . . ." William W. Woodward, *Meet General Grant* (New York: H. Liveright, 1928), quoted in W. E. B. Du Bois, *Black Reconstruction* (New York: Atheneum [1969]), 716.

Page 47: "In 1863 Southerners began to feel . . ." Morison and Commager, *Growth of the American Republic*, 1st ed. (1930), 582–83.

Page 48: "the vindictive Thaddeus Stevens . . ." This and other passages on Reconstruction from Nevins and Commager, *America*, 1st ed. (1942), 218–20.

Page 49: "Agriculture—the economic lifeblood . . ." Bailey, *American Pageant*, 461.

Page 49: "The average ex-slave . . ." Ibid., 463.

Page 50: "The sudden thrusting of the ballot . . ." and subsequent passages. Ibid., 475–78.

Page 51: "The negro was the central figure . . ." Morison and Comager, *Growth of the American Republic*, 1st ed. (1930), 621–22.

Page 51: "Fair-minded Southerners at once . . ." Ibid., 622.

Page 51: "one of the most unpleasant . . ." Ibid., 637.

Page 52: "police unruly and criminal . . ." Ibid., 649.

Page 52: "The resulting state administrations . . ." Ibid., 642.

Page 52: "The historic decision of the Supreme Court . . ." Bailey, *American Pageant*, 938.

Page 53: "While Virginia was thus shooting . . ." Nevins and Commager, *America*, 1st ed. (1942), p. 6.

Page 53: "While Virginia was thus painfully . . ." Nevins and Commager, *America*, 3rd ed. (Oxford: Clarendon Press, 1967), 6.

Page 53: "The American Republic, which is still . . ." Bailey, Kennedy, and Cohen, *American Pageant*, 11th ed. (Boston: Houghton Mifflin, 1998), 4–5.

Page 54: Nevins and Commager add a new section . . . *America*, 3rd ed., 563 ff.

Page 54: Morison and Commager cover much the same ground . . . See Morison and Commager, 5th ed. (New York: Oxford University Press, 1962), 2:966 ff.

Page 54: By the time the eleventh edition of Bailey . . . See Bailey, Kennedy, and Cohen, *American Pageant*, 11th ed., chapters 40 and 41.

Page 54: "The Negro, as Dr. Albert Schweitzer . . ." Morison and Commager, *Growth of the American Republic*, 5th ed. (1962), 525e.

Page 55: "Instances of sadistic cruelty . . ." Ibid., 527.

Page 55: By 1966, Thaddeus Stevens has become . . . Nevins and Commager, *America*, 3rd ed. (1967), 243.

Page 55: "The following excerpt . . ." Bailey, Kennedy, and Cohen, *American Pageant*, 11th ed. (1998), 503.

Page 56: "They were, in many cases incompetent . . ." Nevins and Commager, 3rd ed. (1967), 244.

Page 56: "For almost a century now . . ." Ibid., 243.

Page 56: See Morison and Commager, *Growth of the American Republic*, 2nd ed. (1937), 2:45–49.

Page 57: "There is no entirely satisfactory . . ." Ibid., 594.

Page 57: "negroes and their white allies . . ." Ibid., 46.

Page 57: "Both . . . words are of course heavily loaded . . ." Morison and Commager, *Growth of the American Republic*, 5th ed. (1962), 2:42.

Page 59: "freedom has provided . . ." Eric Foner, *The Story of American Freedom* (New York: W. W. Norton, 1998), Introduction.

Page 59: "By 1800, indentured . . ." Ibid., 19.

Chapter Three

Page 61: "Dramatically the Negro . . ." W. E. B. Du Bois, *The Gift of Black Folk* (New York: Washington Square Press, 1970), 65. (Originally published in 1924.)

Page 61: "I am going to tell this story . . ." W. E. B. Du Bois, "To the Reader," in *Black Reconstruction*, 1969.

Page 63: "Alice Travellor, the mistress . . ." Jacqueline Jones, *American Work* (New York: Norton, 1998), 71.

Page 66: "Africans were in South Carolina from the beginning . . ." Charles Joyner, *Down by the Riverside* (Urbana and Chicago: University of Illinois press, 1985), 13–14.

Page 70: "The connection between American slavery and freedom . . ." Edmund Morgan, *American Slavery, American Freedom* (New York: Norton, 1974), 5, 338.

Page 71: "Thomas Jefferson estimated . . ." John Hope Franklin and Alfred A. Moss, Jr., *From Slavery to Freedom*, 7th ed. (New York: McGraw-Hill, Inc., 1994), 75. (Originally published in 1947.)

Page 76: "It must be borne in mind that . . ." Du Bois, *Black Reconstruction* (1969), 57.

Page 78: "Caddy had been sold . . ." Leon Litwack, *Been in the Storm So Long* (New York: Vintage Books, 1980), 186–87.

Page 79: The letter first appeared in the *Cincinnati Commercial* and was reprinted in the *New York Tribune* of August 22, 1965. It is reproduced here from Litwak, *Been in the Storm*, 333–34.

Page 80: "I never did a day's work . . ." Ibid., 359.

Page 81: "I am tired . . ." Ibid., 358.

Page 81: "The great problem to be solved . . ." See Gerald Jaynes, *Branches without Roots* (New York: Oxford University Press, 1986), 3.

Page 85: "Whites in general believed . . ." Jones, *American Work*, 271–72.

Page 89: "The brutalities meted out . . ." Leon Litwack, *Trouble in Mind* (New York: Knopf, 1998), 288–89.

Page 91: "if a neighborhood is to maintain . . ." Quoted in Melvin Oliver and Thomas Shapiro, *Black Wealth/White Wealth* (New York: Routledge, 1997), 18.

Page 95: Derrick Bell . . . See Derrick Bell, "The Space Traders," in *Faces at the Bottom of the Well* (New York: Basic Books, 1992).

Chapter Four

Page 99: It is time to take a closer look . . . The story of the growth of modern Black Studies programs has been told many times. See, for example, Robert H. Brisbane, *Black Activism: Racial Revolution in the United States, 1954-1970* (Valley Forge, Pa.: Judson Press, 1974), Chapter 10. See also several of the essays in John W. Blassingame, *New Perspectives on Black Studies* (Urbana: University of Illinois Press, 1971), and Maulana Karenga, *Introduction to Black Studies*, 2nd ed. (Los Angeles: University of Sankore Press, 1993), Introduction.

Page 101: "American literature courses meandered . . ." Roger A. Fischer, "Ghetto and Gown: The Birth of Black Studies" in *New Perspectives on Black Studies*, ed. John W. Blassingame, 17–18 (Urbana: University of Illinois Press, 1971).

Page 102: "After several months of determined effort . . ." This and the subsequent quotes come from Craig Foster Robinson and Donald Ogilvie, eds., *Black Studies in the University* (New Haven, Conn.: Yale University Press, 1969). The volume contains the proceedings of the conference held at Yale in 1968. Robinson went on to do graduate work in history, and near the end of his life headed the Carter Woodson Institute at the University of Virginia.

Page 102: "This belated recognition . . ." I owe this reference, and much more besides, to Lawrence W. Levine's splendid book *The Opening of the American Mind* (Boston: Beacon Press, 1996).

Page 105: "Africa proper, as far as History goes back . . ." I take these lines from the translation by J. Sibree of Hegel's *Lectures on the Philosophy of History*, with prefaces by Charles Hegel and the translator, J. Sibree, and a new introduction by Professor C. J. Friedrich, Harvard University (New York: Dover, 1956). They are selected from pages 91–99. For an extensive collection of truly horrible passages gleaned from the writings of the leading figures of the European and American Enlightenment see Emmanuel Chukwudi Eze, ed., *Race and the Enlightenment: A Reader* (Cambridge, Mass.: Blackwell, 1997). It is enough to make a student of modern philosophy weep.

Page 107: "African cultures, Schlesinger tells us . . ." See Levine, *Opening of the American Mind*, 164–65. The quoted passages are from Arthur Schlesinger, *The Disuniting of America* (New York: Norton, 1992); Hugh Trevor-Roper, *The Rise of Christian Europe* (London: Thames and Hudson, 1965); and Lewis Feuer, "From Pluralism to Multiculturalism," *Society* 29 (November/December 1991). I have one bone to pick with Levine. It is entirely unfair to describe Feuer as a philosopher. Although he did, I admit, begin his career as a philosopher, in his mature years, he was a Professor of Sociology. Hegel is quite enough of a burden for philosophy to bear.

Page 108: Europe, Africa, the Near and Middle East . . . For a fascinating discussion of this and other aspects of the old world system of international trade, see Janet Abu-Lughod, *Before World Hegemony: The World System A.D. 1250–1350* (New York: Oxford University Press, 1989). See also Eric Wolf, *Europe and the People without History* (Berkeley: University of California Press, 1982). Wallerstein's theories can be found in *The Modern World System*, volumes 1 (1974) and 2 (1979) (New York: Academic Press).

Page 110: "I am constrained to feel . . ." Arthur Schlesinger, Jr., *The Disuniting of America*, rev. and enlarged ed. (New York: Norton, 1998), 80.

Page 110: "The glorification of the African past . . ." Ibid., 91.

Page 111: "the most complete philosophical totalization . . ." Molefi Kete Asante, *The Afrocentric Idea* (Philadelphia: Temple University Press, 1987), 125. Asante has written or edited a number of books, but this one seems to me to contain his most definitive exposition of the concept of Afrocentricity, or, as he in some places refers to it, Afrocalogy or Afrology.

Page 112: "The preponderant Eurocentric myths . . ." Ibid., 9. Next two quotations, p. 6.

Page 116: "To attract and keep . . ." Nell Irvin Painter, "Black Studies, Black Professors, and the Struggles of Perception," *The Chronicle Review*, December 15, 2000, p. B9.

Page 121: "The great American innovation . . ." Alain Touraine, *The Academic System in American Society* (New York: McGraw Hill, 1974), 33.

A Concluding Word

Page 123: "May I escape the tragicomic predicament . . ." S. Kierkegaard, *Philosophical Fragments, or A Fragment of Philosophy*, trans. David F. Swenson (Princeton, N.J.: Princeton University Press, 1936), 1–2.

THE ORIGINAL SYLLABUS OF FIFTY MAJOR WORKS OF AFRO-AMERICAN STUDIES, IN THE ORDER IN WHICH THE STUDENTS READ THEM THE FIRST YEAR, 1996–97

These were the editions assigned to the students, not necessarily the original versions.

Franklin, John Hope, and Alfred A. Moss, Jr. *From Slavery to Freedom, A History of African Americans.* 7th edition. McGraw-Hill, Inc., 1994.

Meier, August, and Elliott Rudwick. *Black History and the Historical Profession, 1915–1980.* University of Illinois Press, 1986.

Parish, Peter J. *Slavery: History and Historians.* Harper & Row, Publishers, 1989.

Williams, Eric. *Capitalism and Slavery.* University of North Carolina Press, 1944.

Higginbotham, A. Leon, Jr. *In the Matter of Color Race & The American Legal Process: The Colonial Period.* Oxford University Press, 1978.

Kaplan, Sidney, and Emma Nogrady Kaplan. *The Black Presence in the Era of the American Revolution.* Revised edition. University of Massachusetts Press, 1989.

Gates, Henry Louis, Jr., ed. *The Classic Slave Narratives.* Mentor Books. New American Library, 1987.

Gutman, Herbert G. *The Black Family in Slavery and Slavery and Freedom, 1750–1925.* Vintage Books, 1976.

Pease, Jane H., and William H. Pease. *They Who Would Be Free: Blacks' Search for Freedom, 1830–1861.* University of Illinois Press, 1990.

Nash, Gary B. *Forging Freedom: The Formation of Philadelphia's Black Community, 1720–1840.* Harvard University Press, 1988.

Levine, Lawrence W. *Black Culture and Black Consciousness: Afro-American Folk Thought from Slavery to Freedom.* Oxford University Press, 1977.

Fields, Barbara Jeanne. *Slavery and Freedom on the Middle Ground: Maryland During the Nineteenth Century.* Yale University Press, 1985.

Stowe, Harriet Beecher. *Uncle Tom's Cabin, or Life among the Lowly.* Introduction by Ann Douglas. Penguin Books, 1981.

Harper, Frances E. W. *Iola Leroy, or Shadows Uplifted.* Introduction by Frances Foster Smith. Oxford University Press, 1988.

Brown, William Wells. *Clotel, or The President's Daughter.* Introduction and Annotations by William Edward Farrison. Carol Publishing Group, 1995.

Chesnutt, Charles W. *The Conjure Woman and Other Conjure Tales.* Edited with an Introduction by Richard H. Brodhead. Duke University Press, 1993.

Foner, Eric. *Reconstruction: America's Unfinished Revolution, 1863–1877.* Harper & Row, 1988.

Litwack, Leon F. *Been in the Storm So Long: The Aftermath of Slavery.* Vintage Books, 1979.

Painter, Nell Irvin. *Exodusters: Black Migration to Kansas after Reconstruction.* Alfred A. Knopf, 1977.

Jones, Jacqueline. *Labor of Love, Labor of Sorrow: Black Women, Work, and the Family from Slavery to the Present.* Vintage Books, 1995.

Giddings, Paula. *When and Where I Enter: The Impact of Black Women on Race and Sex in America.* Morrow, 1984.

Walker, Margaret. *Jubilee.* Bantam Books, 1967.

Gaines, Ernest J. *The Autobiography of Miss Jane Pittman.* Dial Press, 1971.

Du Bois, W. E. B. *The Souls of Black Folks.* In *Three Negro Classics.* Introduction by John Hope Franklin. Avon Books, 1965.

Washington, Booker T. *Up from Slavery.* In *Three Negro Classics.* Introduction by John Hope Franklin. Avon Books, 1965.

Aptheker, Herbert. *A Documentary History of the Negro People in the United States.* Vol. 5. Carol Publishing Company, 1993.

Locke, Alain, ed. *The New Negro: Voices of the Harlem Renaissance.* Atheneum, 1992.

Johnson, James Weldon. *Autobiography of an Ex-Colored Man.* In *Three Negro Classics.* Introduction by John Hope Franklin. Avon Books, 1965.

Bell, Bernard. *The Afro-American Novel and Its Tradition.* University of Massachusetts Press, 1987.

Baker, Huston, Jr. *The Journey Back: Issues in Black Literature and Criticism.* University of Chicago Press, 1980.

Hine, Darlene Clark, ed. *The State of Afro-American History: Past, Present, and Future.* Louisiana State University Press, 1986.

McKay, Claude. *Home to Harlem.* Northeastern University Press, 1987.

Toomer, Jean. *Cane.* Introduction by Darwin T. Turner. Liveright, 1975.

The Negro Caravan: Writings by American Negroes. Selected and edited by Sterling A. Brown, Arthur P. Davis, and Ulysses Lee. Citadel Press, 1941.

Fauset, Jessie Redmon. *Plum Bun: A Novel without a Moral.* Introduction by Deborah E. McDowell. Beacon Press, 1990.

Hurston, Zora Neale. *Jonah's Gourd Vine.* With a new foreword by Rita Dove. Harper Perennial, 1990.

Hurston, Zora Neale. *Their Eyes Were Watching God.* With a new foreword by Mary Helen Washington. Harper Perennial, 1990.

Woodson, Carter G. *The Mis-Education of the Negro.* Africa World Press, 1990.

Kelley, Robin D. G. *Hammer and Hoe: Alabama Communists during the Great Depression.* University of North Carolina Press, 1990.

Rosengarten, Theodore. *All God's Dangers: The Life of Nate Shaw.* Vintage Books, 1989.

Hughes, Langtson. *I Wonder As I Wander: An Autobiographical Journey.* Introduction by Arnold Rampersad. Hill and Wang, 1993.

Drake, St. Clair, and Horace A. Cayton. *Black Metropolis: A Study of Negro Life in a Northern City*. Revised and enlarged edition, with an Introduction by Richard Wright. University of Chicago Press, 1970.

Wright, Richard. *Uncle Tom's Children*. Introduction by Richard Yarborough. Harper Perennial, 1965.

Wright, Richard. *Native Son*. Introduction, "How 'Bigger' was born," by the author. Harper and Row, 1940.

Himes, Chester. *If He Hollers Let Him Go*. Foreword by Graham Hodges. Thunder's Mouth Press, 1986.

Ellison, Ralph. *Invisible Man*. Vintage Books, 1981.

Baldwin, James. *Go Tell It on the Mountain*. Dell Publishing Company, 1953.

Baldwin, James. *The Price of the Ticket: Collected Non-Fiction, 1948–1985*. St. Martin's Press, 1985.

King, Martin Luther, Jr. *Stride toward Freedom: The Montgomery Story*. Harper, 1958.

Kluger, Richard. *Simple Justice: The History of Brown v. Board of Education and Black America's Struggle for Equality*. Vintage Books, 1977.

Moody, Anne. *Coming of Age in Mississippi*. Dell Publishing Company, 1968.

BOOKS BY ROBERT PAUL WOLFF

Kant's Theory of Mental Activity. 1963.
A Critique of Pure Tolerance, with Barrington Moore, Jr., and Herbert Marcuse. 1965.
Political Man and Social Man, edited with Introduction. 1966.
Kant: A Collection of Critical Essays, with Introduction. 1967.
The Poverty of Liberalism. 1968.
The Ideal of the University. 1969.
The Essential Hume, with Introduction. 1969.
Kant: Foundations of the Metaphysics of Morals: Text and Commentary, with Introduction. 1969.
In Defense of Anarchism, Hardcover and Paperback. 1970.
Ten Great Works of Philosophy, with Introduction. 1970.
Philosophy: A Modern Encounter. 1971.
The Rule of Law. 1971.
Styles of Political Action in America. 1972.
The Autonomy of Reason: A Commentary on Kant's Groundwork of the Metaphysic of Morals. 1973.
1984 Revisited: Prospects for American Politics. 1973.
About Philosophy. 1976.
Understanding Rawls. 1977.
Introductory Philosophy. 1979.
Understanding Marx: A Reconstruction and Critique of "Capital." 1985.
Moneybags Must Be So Lucky: On the Literary Structure of "Capital." 1988.

INDEX OF NAMES

Autobiography of an Ex-White Man is an intensely personal meditation on the nature of America by a White philosopher who joined a Black Studies department and found his understanding of the world transformed by the experience. The book begins with an autobiographical narrative of the events leading up to Wolff's transfer from a philosophy department to the W. E. B. Du Bois Department of Afro-American Studies at the University of Massachusetts, and his experiences in the department with his new colleagues, all of whom had come to academia from the Civil Rights Movement of the 1960s. Wolff discovered that the apparently simple act of moving across campus to a new department in a new building worked a startling change in the way he saw himself, his university, and his country. Reading as widely as possible to bring himself up to speed on his new field of academic responsibility, Wolff realized that his picture of American history and culture was undergoing an irreversible metamorphosis. America, he discovered, has from its inception been a land both of freedom and of bondage—freedom for the few, and then for those who are White, bondage at first for the many, and then for those who are not White. Slavery is thus not an aberration, an accident, a peculiar institution; it is the essence and core of the American experience.

Robert Paul Wolff is Professor of Afro-American Studies at the University of Massachusetts-Amherst.